Advance Praise for
Bet You Didn't See That One Coming

"I highly recommend *Bet You Didn't See That One Coming* to anyone interested in the ways and means of the Trump phenomenon and its consequences for America. This is not just another campaign book. It is an entertaining analysis of what happened in 2016, and why."

—The Honorable Dave Camp, Former Chairman,
House Ways & Means Committee

"Good to have a serious conservative analyze without blinders the strengths and weaknesses of President Trump's politics and rhetoric. This work provides serious conservative perspectives on what fair presidential observers should make of a politically inexperienced and stylistically inelegant president who challenges the domestic and foreign policy perspectives of an immediately prior hardened leftist but charming president."

—Richard E. Vatz, PhD, Towson University Distinguished Professor

"Governor Ehrlich's fourth book presents a fascinating analysis of the Obama record. An accurate and informative interpretation of how the excesses of Barack Obama's progressivism led to the election of President Trump. A must-read for anyone attempting to figure out what on earth is going on in Trump's Washington!"

—The Honorable David McIntosh, President, Club for Growth

"Robert Ehrlich is both a practitioner and an observer; a politician and an analyst. That is a potent combination, on display in this book. He knows whereof he speaks. His words have special authority."

—Jay Nordlinger, Senior Editor, *National Review*

"Governor Bob Ehrlich is that rare kind of straight-talking sensible Republican, and he's from Maryland. *Bet You Didn't See That One Coming* shares his unique conservative perspective on how power shifted from Obama to Trump. Governor Ehrlich explains where we are today and what the future portends. *Bet You Didn't See That One Coming* is a good read!"

—Ed Feulner, President, The Heritage Foundation

"Bob Ehrlich has scaled the political peaks—state legislator, Congressman, Maryland Governor—without ever going establishment. In his latest book, he casts a cool discerning eye on our two most recent presidents, and how the defects of Barack Obama led to the election of Donald Trump."

—Michael Barone, *Washington Examiner*; American Enterprise Institute; founding coauthor, *The Almanac of American Politics*

"Governor Ehrlich's new book is a cogent analysis of how Donald Trump's victory has challenged Obama's progressive agenda. This well-written book provides readers with rich insights into a very different political leader and his unique ways."

—Governor Haley Barbour

Bet You Didn't See That One Coming

Bet You Didn't See That One Coming

★ ★ ★ ★ ★

Obama, Trump, and the End of
Washington's Regular Order

Governor Bob Ehrlich

A POST HILL PRESS BOOK

Bet You Didn't See That One Coming
Obama, Trump, and the End of Washington's Regular Order
© 2018 Bob Ehrlich
All Rights Reserved

ISBN: 978-1-68261-754-0
ISBN (eBook): 978-1-68261-755-7

Cover Design by Tricia Principe, principedesign.com

Author's Note: Some material has been slightly edited from the original material for consistency and clarification.

Post Hill
PRESS

New York • Nashville
posthillpress.com

Published in the United States of America

Table of Contents

Introduction

Did *I* see that one coming?

Honest answer: no...and yes.

I can count on one hand the people who can lay serious claim to the "without a doubt Trump will win" club; I am not one of them. Yours truly adopted more of a "it will be close, but she should still pull it out" view.

It seems my cardholding membership in the GOP establishment (state legislator, U.S. Representative, Governor of Maryland, and partner in a major DC law firm) held me back from truly crossing into "Believe Land." Still, I had seen too much of the grassroots up close and personal to simply dismiss what Trump had accomplished. I knew *all* the intensity was with the outsider, but Republicans had been burned too often in the past by unmet expectations from the Rust Belt: Michigan, Wisconsin, and (especially) Pennsylvania.

What happened leading up to Election Day will be analyzed in minute detail for decades. Countless books will be written (some are already on bestseller lists), but I did not simply want to write another campaign story. It had to be larger—as much about why Obama's transformative presidency ended the way it did as why Trump was able to pull off the unthinkable. Understanding how one led to other is the only way to grasp the magnitude of Election 2016 and the implications for our future.

So *Bet You Didn't See That One Coming* is far more than a collection of essays in the Age of Trump. Each chapter is arranged to provide the reader with a coherent commentary on American economic and cultural values from Obama's second term through the first year of the Trump presidency. Phrased another way, the reader is taken from "You didn't build that" to a "basket of deplorables" to "Damn straight I built that."

Such a path presented myriad storylines. Fortunately, my previously published columns centered on issues that helped illuminate the great change. Accordingly, chapters specific to the end of the Obama era, the Trump phenomenon and *modus operandi*, the politics and economics of job creation, the plague of urban blight and its resulting despair, progressivism's rhetorical infatuation with speech control, and the fun of writing humor pieces that amuse me (and hopefully you—but not so much lefty critics suffering from decidedly limited senses of humor) to no end are included in the coming pages.

* * *

The once inconceivable went down around 11:30 p.m. on November 8, 2016. Overnight, everything changed. European-style social welfare-ism was suddenly out. A Trump-styled version of American nationalism was suddenly in. The contrast was dramatic in ways large and small.

Our story begins with a second-term Obama intent on legacy building but reduced to unilateral executive actions—many of which are being overturned by the courts. A significantly diminished Democratic minority in Congress is an afterthought, its ranks having been devastated during Obama's tenure. But the true-believing, "stop the oceans rising" president refused to go quietly into the night. Instead, Obama-style progressivism would go out with an arrogant thud. While slow growth continued to strangle the working class, a barrage of last-minute regulations spewed out of the federal bureaucracy—many intended to tie the hands of the incoming Trump administration. Approved pipelines were shut down. Millions of additional acres of western land were deemed national monuments and taken off the tax rolls. Overseas, a last-minute UN sucker punch at Israel's West Bank settlements was followed by the stealthy authorization of a couple hundred million dollars of American taxpayer money to the Palestinian Authority (ultimately revoked by Trump). And publicly announced, on-time departure schedules (independent of situations on the ground) from world hotspots were contributing to all kinds of provocations from anti-American miscreants in the Middle East, Eastern Europe, and Asia.

Inauguration Day brought huge television ratings and plenty of red Trump baseball caps to the National Mall. Thousands of heartland deplorables showed up to party. A highly anticipated inaugural address was quintessential Trump. An "America first" worldview was announced with the usual Trumpian subtlety of a Mack truck. Republicans smiled and Democrats frowned. This was an earth-shattering changing of the guard.

The next day, radical feminists and assorted other members of the grievance industry gathered in large numbers (up to 500,000) to march and shout ugly chants. Hollywood libs threatened to leave the country. Leftist intellectuals fretted. The media quickly reorganized and began to dig in for the long haul. Meanwhile, in flyover country, millions of marginalized Americans began to think they finally had a voice within the power corridors of Washington, DC. It was *their* time, against all odds, made possible by a most unlikely political neophyte and leader.

As events unfolded and days turned into weeks and weeks into months, angst-ridden Obama-ites began to organize relentlessly and with purpose. Indeed, as their frustration played out nightly on our television screens, the opposition became a caricature—and easily diagnosed in their abbreviated three-step anger management program.

Stage one was short-lived but memorable—the stunned, tearful reactions on the urban coasts as one after another of the "Blue Wall" Rust Belt states turned red during the evening hours of November 8, 2016.

Stage two came with the protests: students, professors, feminists, illegal aliens, community organizers, professional demonstrators, and just plain old run-of-the-mill disgruntled Americans all stepped forward to register their disgust with Donald Trump and his ways. "He's a fascist" was a favorite indictment—this from many of the same demonstrators ever ready to shout down a conservative or right-wing speaker on a college campus.

Finally, stage three arrived with the building blocks of a permanent resistance. The rhetoric herein was indeed unique, as many of the rank and file turned to nullification in refusing to accept November's outcome, a logical reaction from those who believe only right-wingers are consigned to accept election results. Progressivism's steadfast belief in its ownership of the moral high ground has its advantages.

Nevertheless, a resistance movement (including major print and electronic news organizations) in the aftermath of a free and fair election in the most successful democracy the world has ever seen made for a unique narrative. Media gleefully reported the anti-Trump storylines. One day it was a rogue group of federal workers said to be undermining Trump administration initiatives (including highly placed professionals within our intelligence agencies); the next it was hundreds of mayors and local executives doubling down to resist federal immigration law. Newspaper front pages began editorializing their "straight news" stories, and network news focused on anti-Trump story after anti-Trump story.

And then came something the American public rarely experiences: the new ex-president and former community organizer tweeting encouraging messages to the rabidly agitated and offering to lend his expertise to a new generation of social justice activists. No modern president had dared to assume such an audacious (yes, you can say it) role. One thing was perfectly clear: The man who promised to transform America was not yet satisfied with his life's work. Going radio silent was not in his DNA, elections to the contrary be damned!

Introduction

The beginning of the Trump era was rocky, frenetic, sensational history. A peaceful transfer of power was followed by anything but peace. A *very* different leader with a very different approach now called the shots.

This tome tells the story of the monumental clash that ensued—a conflict that will continue for years to come. The accompanying brutality has been difficult to watch. The great progressive experiment had been stopped in its tracks. A decade of rapidly changing social mores and explosive government growth (and reach) was by the boards. The country had moved right, albeit cautiously.

The sudden change was dramatic but unique. Donald Trump was certainly not Ralph Reed and a "moral majority" redux, but more Arnold Schwarzenegger in *Terminator 2*. Recall that that was the *good* Arnold—still intent on blowing up anything and everything that stood in his way.

A deeply divided country reacted, predictably. Half of us stood up and applauded; the other half stood up to protest. You will soon figure out this book is written from the perspective of the former, but with some understanding of the latter's frustrations.

Obama II and Trump I *are* oil and water. The two were never meant to mix, but their toxic interaction is enormously important history to understand.

CHAPTER 1

What Just Happened?
Election Pre- and Postmortems

Picture the former Governor of Maryland (that's me) sitting at a long picnic-type table in an American Legion auxiliary hall in Ashland, New Hampshire, during the spring of 2015. I was there at the invitation of my friend, JP Marzullo, a former Maryland constituent who had migrated north years earlier and who was now engaged in the business of getting me; my new book, *Turning Point*; and my views better known in the state of New Hampshire. Despite media speculation to the contrary, this was *not* a "listening tour" campaign visit, but rather one of a dozen stops in the Granite State arranged for the above-described reasons.

An otherwise unmemorable night included being introduced to Donald Trump's newly designated New Hampshire "guy," Zach Montanaro. This was the point in the presidential cycle when declared and soon-to-be-declared candidates employed such representatives "in the field." Their presence showed a seriousness of purpose and an understanding of the central importance of the "First in the Nation" New Hampshire primary. Zach was a nice enough young fellow and certainly knew New Hampshire and its politics. But I could not judge how serious a campaign he intended to wage. After all, this was a time when Marco Rubio, Jeb Bush, and Scott Walker were dominating the GOP polls. Donald Trump was a single-digit afterthought. To boot, spaghetti dinners in front of small and sometimes hostile crowds is a long way (on the "fun scale") from *Celebrity Apprentice*, let alone Mar-a-Lago. And there are endless such dinners for serious presidential candidates. I, for one, could not envision a frenetic Manhattan real estate mogul putting up with such a schedule. My dominant thought at the time was that the Trump campaign was engaged in more farcical adventure than actual campaign. "At least Zach will be paid" was my takeaway from the night.

Now fast-forward approximately six months, to the campaign headquarters of the Naples, Florida, Republican Party. A packed office of over one hundred volunteer GOP activists sat and listened to my pitch for *Turning Point* and Ohio Governor John Kasich, my friend and former budget committee chairman. It was a wonderful evening with newly minted friends, but my mind's eye was focused on the approximately dozen women wearing Trump T-shirts and appearing to suffer from major consternation every time I took issue with or appeared to criticize their candidate. These "Trumpers" paid close attention to my words; the smallest real or perceived slight directed at Mr. Trump quickly metastasized into something far larger—i.e., a none-too-subtle code utilized by Republican Party establishment types, intended to slow the progress of the Trump bandwagon. The Trump supporters' lack of a sense of humor (or balance) regarding DJT, and their insistence that he was the *only* Republican capable of defeating Hillary Clinton, left strong impressions from this and a half dozen other book tour trips to the Sunshine State.

Yet another deeply ingrained memory of 2016 centers on *establishment* Washington's attitude toward Trump and his candidacy. My association with one of the world's leading law firms (King & Spalding) provided me with a front-row seat to the awkwardness of *The Donald Meets Washington* show. And believe me—precious few of Washington's power brokers thought this would be a long-running engagement.

Most of this crowd bought into two of the most prominent "Never Trump" talking points: that Trump was too polarizing a public figure to win a general election and/or that a "demographic death warrant" (not my phrase) had descended on an old, lily-white GOP.

This well-entrenched, permanent power structure (K Street lobbying and law firms, professional associations, and mainstream media networks) is reliably left-leaning in normal circumstances, but this time it was *totally* in the tank for Hillary Clinton, relentless scandals and consistent deceptions notwithstanding. No Trump comment or aside went without hypercritical analysis—and typically some degree of condemnation—especially unapologetic appeals to American nationalism viewed as socially unacceptable nativism by the progressive intelligentsia. During these months I lost count of the number of conversations I had that began and ended with the prediction "Trump can't win"—this despite polls that reflected consistently high Clinton unfavorables in blue-leaning battleground states.

I recount these recollections to remind you that despite his demonstrated business successes and long-running celebrity, Donald J. Trump was little more than a punch line during the early stages of Campaign 2016; that a major factor in Trump's early success was the vacuum created by a persistent enthusiasm gap for the campaign of Hillary Clinton; that the billionaire reality TV star and real estate developer with the lavish lifestyle was able to close the deal with America's white working-class voters (including many women) *early* in the cycle; and that the base of both party establishments never did get around to taking the temperature and depth of flyover America's discontent with the slow growth and limited-horizons path of the Obama era.

This last point will be the focus of scholarly analysis for years. For the Democrats, it will serve as a reminder (if anyone bothers to look) of just how out of touch our elites are with Middle America. But this conclusion is neither new nor shocking. The two sides of our economic and cultural divide engage daily. That one pays little attention to where the other is coming from is a familiar indictment.

Far more interesting will be the investigations from the right vis-à-vis the rise of Donald Trump. Talk about an uninvited guest. Here is the guy who shows up late, eats your food, insults the other guests, and then tells his friends what a terrible party you hosted. Hosts tend to dismiss such guests as an anomaly, much as the Republican leadership treated Trump in the early days. But this dismissal came with a cost—the party leadership whiffed on what its own base was thinking. And they still won!

The following essays examine how and why a once unimaginable Trump movement began and generated such momentum, starting with a look back at the stage set by the Obama administration's progressive activism.

A Retrospective on the Obama Years Seven Years In…

January 26, 2016, *The Weekly Standard*

It has been seven years since the election of our first black president. Seven years since a supposed post-partisan (even post-racial) era was to begin.

But expectations were too high, especially among those who were certain the country's major problems were racially based. The pundits got it wrong. "Hope" and "change" turned out to be mere campaign slogans. America's racial divide has deepened. And a previously slobbering media has (unhappily) reported on a sharply divided (and coarsened) America.

Such naïve expectations had no connection to reality in the first place. State Senator Obama and United States Senator Obama was indeed articulate, charismatic, and charming—but also hyperpartisan and ultra-liberal. Nobody can reasonably say they're surprised that the same mindset and philosophical approach followed him to the White House.

Yet, the promised "transformation" of America's economy and culture proceeds apace—with too little attention paid to its progress.

As America staggers toward the end of Obama's second term, this observer offers the following report.

Tax & Spend

One of the weakest recoveries in the post-war period (labor participation remains historically low), a "shovel-less," oversold stimulus, massive tax hikes, and explosive spending define the Obama economic record.

The result is a federal debt soaring toward $20 trillion, $9 trillion of which will have been added during Obama's tenure. Remember when Senator Obama labeled George W. Bush's $4 trillion debt "irresponsible" and "unpatriotic"? Well, apparently, neither does he.

Neither Democrats nor Republicans are willing to address the budget mess. One party abhors any action to rein in government spending; the other talks a good game but almost always fails to deliver. The public expresses little outrage. Few Americans imagine a budget reckoning. But that day will come sooner rather than later thanks to the mad spending spree of Barack Obama and his acolytes.

Housing

Recent progressive rhetoric brings to mind the market-bending arguments that led to the great recession of 2008–12. To wit, everyone should own a home, regardless of credit rating, income, or debt burden. And to the extent that some lending institutions fail to board the easy credit bandwagon, they get personally demonized as "redliners" and "racists."

The Obama administration's more recent attempt to revisit subprime credit should be closely monitored, and resisted. Despite representations to the contrary, the laws of supply and demand are not subject to change—even in Washington, DC.

Which brings us to the recent story of New York Mayor Bill de Blasio's attempt to leverage New York banks into a more "socially conscious" (read: easy money) lending regime. Fortunately, a federal judge remembered in early August to read the law and held this latest local outrage from the dangerous Mr. de Blasio unconstitutional.

Another beauty from Obama's Department of Housing and Urban Development concerns proposed rules to preempt local zoning where the Washington social engineers see insufficient amounts of racial integration. Yes, you read that correctly. The federal government has calculated the "correct" racial and economic mix for your neighborhood. And to think entire generations of us were raised to believe "fair housing" meant that every American got to live where he or she wants to live regardless of what you look like or where you came from—if you can afford it.

Higher Education

America's college campuses have always been a home field for the left. It's a rule of life that socialism, progressivism, and liberalism tend to flourish in an environment where tenure reigns and where intellectual adventurism is supposed to blossom without the burden(s) of waking early, going to work, and paying the bills.

But today's college scene is a bridge too far. Seems not a day goes by without a media report of some college professor gone off the progressive deep end. Indeed, we are becoming desensitized to stories of "speech codes," "bias-free guides," "safe zones," and "trigger warnings." And it's all to do with an aggrieved, fearful left now turned against free speech. (A Rutgers University "Bias Prevention and Education Committee" told students, "There's no such thing as free speech.") The historic demands for freedom that characterized the great American civil rights movement are now a relic of the 1960s.

Such was a traditional notion of higher education until a new brand of militant progressivism began to take root. This virulent movement has little in common with that bygone and more intellectually curious era. Today's movement is more akin to a rhetorical gulag, wherein speech codes rule and an "offense-less" culture is the goal. This is the non-engagement left, where one runs to a "safe zone" in order to escape those with whom you disagree. And please check your sense of humor (and history) at the door.

Worse, a new wave of student-brats is more than willing to take over a dean/president's office to make its point. After all, the movement is infused with the Clinton/Obama/Alinsky doctrine of "nefarious means justify progressive ends"—interpreted here as the willing degradation and embarrassment of those of insufficient sensitivity. Do you wonder how these coddled children will react when there is no sympathetic college counselor around to hold their hand? So do I.

That the movement has enjoyed great success is beyond question. Cultural attitudes toward wealth inequality, American exceptionalism, women in combat, gay marriage, immigration enforcement, gender identity, and religious freedom have undergone a profound leftward shift.

Simply put, "the marketplace of ideas" has disappeared. You don't need to look further than your local college or university to understand the why. You don't need to look further than your family dinner table to find a place where the trend can be stopped.

Income Inequality

Some people have more money and make more money than others. This inequality is a byproduct of many factors, including talent, intellect, work ethic, birth circumstances, and market capitalism.

But economic fundamentals are ignored in the era of income inequality hysterics. Witness the recent labor-organized protests over a higher federal minimum wage. Progressives from coast to coast adopted the mantra. In response, dozens of states and municipalities raised their local minimum wage. Yet, progressive theory cannot transform marginal labor into skilled labor. And so the non-partisan Congressional Budget Office reported on what fast food chain CEOs have long promised: Higher mandated wages mean fewer jobs and more automation. Alas, there is no union representing the newly unemployed.

The anti-income inequality movement continues to gain traction. And nowhere is the ascendant concept more pronounced than in the rhetoric of Barack Obama, he of "spread the wealth" and "you didn't build that" fame. Guess a record 100 million Americans now receiving some form of government assistance is not enough.

Such rhetorical attacks on old-fashioned American capitalism would have constituted political death for most Democrats in the age from Reagan to Bush but no longer. "Occupy Wall Street" may have failed because it forgot to shower and be socially presentable, but the smooth, articulate community organizer practiced essentially the same philosophy and won two presidential elections. Today, committed class warriors such as Bernie Sanders and Elizabeth Warren preach identity politics and draw large crowds. And the Democratic National Committee openly supports "Black Lives Matter," which should tell you all you need to know about where one of America's two major political parties and a substantial part of the electorate reside these days.

Health Care

It is not surprising that the one-size-fits-all, federally imposed reform known as "Obamacare" has significantly damaged health care delivery in America. Indeed, the national media regularly reports critical stories and exposés that depict the law as oversold and underperforming. What else is there to conclude in the wake of insurance premium sticker shock, higher deductibles, reduced consumer choice, co-op failures, sign-up shortfalls, medical device industry layoffs, and the rapid demise of independent medical practices?

The illuminating testimony of Professor Jonathan Gruber affirmed what many of us suspected: that the architects of Obamacare took great pains to increase the bill's complexity and hide its true costs. Nevertheless, the legislation's deep flaws are now painfully obvious to those unfortunate folks who bought the president's promises of "you can keep your doctor" and "a per family savings of $2,500"!

Years of debate have now yielded what should be a commonly accepted conclusion: Anti-choice, anti-market government programs invariably underperform. The experience of American consumers with the latest such experiment should make it easier to explain how market-based alternatives generate better results. Such a task will fall to the next Republican-held White House.

Global Warming

College professors who challenge the concept of man-made global warming put their careers at risk. Recall the ranking Democrat on the House Natural Resources Committee, Sheldon Whitehouse, who initiated an "investigation" of climate scientists and professors expressing contrarian views by sending letters of inquiry to their respective university presidents. Likewise, politicians who question the (often subjective) science become the targets of hostile media types. When inappropriate data manipulation by climate scientists is exposed, the story dies. And the president of the United States is fond of ostracizing those who challenge the science or one of his regulatory remedies.

A share of the blame belongs to conservatives who have allowed themselves to be labeled "climate change deniers," when the science reflects constant temperature change on earth. A more accurate policy statement could have referenced the earth's constantly changing temperature while noting that temperature modeling is subjective and often subject to error.

Suffice it to say that climate politics is a perfect vehicle for the anti-growth, limited-horizon policies of the left. After all, slower growth necessarily follows unilateral disarmament on fossil fuels.

American Exceptionalism

"I believe in American exceptionalism, just as I suspect that the Brits believe in British exceptionalism and the Greeks believe in Greek exceptionalism." (Barack Obama to Edward Luce, *Financial Times*, April 4, 2009.)

This not-so-subtle dig at American exceptionalism falls directly in line with Barack Obama's anti-imperial mindset. His worldview presupposes an America wherein the limits of its military might translate to a "leading from behind" approach to the world's hot spots. For Barack Obama, exiting stage left means avoiding wars of attrition—the central promise of his first campaign.

Yet the same approach allows for the persistence of all flavors of dictator—strongmen to fill the vacuums left by a retreating superpower. The familiar cliché applies: Power does abhor a vacuum. But such results are perfectly acceptable in light of the president's favorite paradigm: Either the U.S. pulls back or there will be war. Such is the familiar narrative of an anti-war activist. Observers of U.S. policy on Ukraine, Syria, and Iran will recognize this trademark Obama talking point.

Race & Ethnicity

Some disaffected conservative Republicans cast a vote for Barack Obama in 2008, despite his down-the-line progressive voting record during his time as a legislator. These individuals were simply done with the Bush-era GOP. Candidate Obama benefitted from this temporary insanity. He also benefited after the election from a renewed sense of national pride. A serious color barrier had been broken. A better racial future was in sight. What more positive statement could be made about America's evolving culture?

Fast-forward to America circa 2015, when a *New York Times* poll found 57 percent of respondents believed race relations are "generally bad," as opposed to 37 percent who responded "generally good." Five years ago, the same question in the same poll found 61 percent good, 33 percent bad. But the Obama era has been "opportunity missed." Every issue is not about race—yet practitioners of the art try to make it so. The bottom line: The Obama/Holder era has shifted race relations in the wrong direction. Today, major Democratic candidates for president apologize for stating that "all lives matter."

Regulation

Remember when the American left's dominant fear was an imperial presidency? Yet today the silence is deafening as an army of appointed bureaucrats and an imperial executive repeatedly bypass the people's elected representatives.

The National Labor Relations Board has morphed into a wholly owned subsidiary of the AFL-CIO. This critical regulator has in turn imprinted organized labor's agenda on the private sector, a remarkable turn of events given labor's ever-declining share of the American workforce. Outside the workplace, Obama's unilateral directive to grant legal status to four million illegal immigrants was unprecedented. So was the "guidance" to allow non-Obamacare insurance plans to be offered in the private insurance marketplace for an additional two years. Only the federal courts have stopped Obama's unilateral rewriting of religious freedom protections granted by law. And the EPA's attempts at expanding the reach of the Clean Air Act are seemingly endless. Lawless? No—the courts have regularly narrowed or defeated such end runs. An imperial mindset? Yes.

National Security

A politically correct "unserious-ness" is an appropriate description of Obama's national security doctrine.

Recall the failure to bomb ISIS-held strategic oil fields that finance the terror army for fear of environmental impact; an immigration policy under which federal agencies fail to examine social media postings of potentially dangerous immigrants; an administration-wide refusal to use the phrase "Islamic terrorists"; a flippant presidential dismissal of ISIS as the "JV squad" while intelligence reports reflected otherwise; posting crooner James Taylor to represent the United States at a Paris unity rally of world leaders; famously playing eighteen holes after acknowledging the torture and burning of a captured Jordanian fighter pilot; Attorney General Loretta Lynch's claim that her first post–San Bernardino priority was discouraging backlash against Muslims; promising and then ignoring a consequential response to Bashar al-Assad's use of weapons of mass destruction in Syria; Secretary of State John Kerry's promise of "an unbelievably small, limited kind of effort" once Assad's WMD line was crossed; the dismissal of the Fort Hood terror killings as "workplace violence"; contending that Syrian refugees are comprehensively vetted while the president's own national security agencies say otherwise; the persistent application of moral equivalence rhetoric in the Palestinian-Israeli conflict; an aggressive rhetorical campaign to weaken (and ultimately defeat) a sitting Israeli prime minister; and a spectacularly weak response to Russian aggression in Ukraine.

On the Other Hand

Alas, the hoped-for transformation is incomplete. Despite a full-court press, Obama's progressive onslaught has failed to move the country further left in a number of important respects. The resistance is real, and not confined to angry Republicans. A prolonged malaise—fear that the American dream is in decline—is the foundation. A broken immigration system, the demise of skilled blue-collar jobs, and the reality of radical Islam provide context. Herewith, a sampling of issues that have proven resistant to Obama-era overtures.

School Choice

The administration has repeatedly sought to defund "opportunity scholarships" in the District of Columbia. Eric Holder's Justice Department sued the State of Louisiana for providing private vouchers to poor black students. And who can forget New York Mayor Bill de Blasio's attempt to increase the rent paid by the city's public charter schools?

But the forces of entrenchment are losing this one. In California, of all places, parents now get to "fire" underperforming schools. Successful public charter schools are multiplying, as are residential charters. And private vouchers are back in vogue.

There is serious movement here. It is the result of too much dysfunction, too many lost kids, too many limited futures. And it is led in part by African Americans from America's inner cities.

School Curriculum

Some of you may recall last year's (2015) proposed College Board guidelines for the AP U.S. history test. (The College Board is the corporation that publishes advanced placement courses and exams.) It was progressive revisionism in all its anti-American glory, including the usual charges of imperialism, nativism, sexism, racism, ethnocentrism, and other "isms."

But the proposed changes were met with significant opposition in red-state legislatures. Some called for the replacement of the board's guidelines. All of this has now led to a revised work product playing to positive reviews on the right and cries of anguish from the left. Even the Founding Fathers are now pictured in a positive light in educational materials. This is progress.

Gun Control

The man who promised he only needs a telephone and a pen to degrade a couple of hundred years of constitutional constraints has found it impossible to pass a federal gun control bill.

The preemptor-in-chief has been quite vocal in his frustration. After all, what modern politician is more adept at using periodic mass shootings to push for yet additional federal control over gun rights?

But even a majority Democratic Congress rejected the president's entreaties. It seems there are a few remaining Democrats representing "flyover districts" where gun control is not seen as a tonic for what ails us, but more like a prescription for defeat in the next general election.

Even the recent and well-publicized executive action on guns represents a minimalist approach, as only a small percentage of individuals who sell firearms on the private market will be affected. Public reaction has been oh-so-predictable: Liberals feel better, conservatives are angry, and gun sales have gone through the roof. We have seen this movie before.

The deadliest domestic terror attack since 9/11 and other periodic terror episodes do not help the president's cause. A public that supports the Second Amendment most certainly does not believe this is an appropriate time to disarm.

Immigration

This one may be a bit of a stretch. Democrats have advanced two-tier driver's licenses, in-state college tuition, sanctuary cities, and all types of welfare benefits on behalf of illegal aliens for years. For this, they have been handsomely rewarded at the polls—especially in blue states.

But that was prior to the mass child migration of 2014, high-profile crimes committed by sanctuary city–protected offenders—and Donald Trump.

Put aside Trump's gratuitous insults and hyperbole for a moment, and even the inconsistencies and ad hominem attacks on his opponents. His central premise is impossible to dismiss: No sovereignty equals no country.

Mitt Romney's self-deportation plan may have cost him an election. Now Trump has doubled down. No one can predict the ultimate outcome. One thing is for sure: Many voters have grown mighty frustrated with porous borders, a broken immigration system, and the unwillingness of politicians from both parties to fix it.

Agency Fees

A foundation of the public sector's union-organizing strength (held constitutional in 1977) is likely to be overturned by the Supreme Court. Such is the media judgment after hostile questioning by the court's sometimes conservative majority. The stakes are indeed high: Unions that lose the ability to collect fees from non-union members see membership rolls and money plummet, which is a huge blow to organized labor and their Democratic Party beneficiaries.

Water in the Desert

Just when the utter absurdity of contemporary political correctness is about to wear you down completely, along comes a story to remind us all is not lost...yet.

First, two caveats: One, my Baltimore roots do not make me a fan of any team from Pittsburgh; and two, I understand where some parents may view the return of athletic trophies as a bit over the line.

Nevertheless, positive reaction to Pittsburgh Steelers linebacker James Harrison's decision to return "participation" trophies "awarded" to his sons is encouraging. A majority of Americans still like to compete and want to win. These folks understand that God invented scoreboards for a reason. Those contrarian parents of a certain progressive mind-set might also recall that try as they might to let everyone "feel good" about participation, kids really do keep score. Just ask them.

Lies and Videotapes

June 9, 2016, *Washington Examiner*

For those of you still wondering how the Obama era could turn the country so left so fast, it's time to stop your analysis. The answer is reflected in our daily headlines: Obama progressives will do or say *anything* to secure their agenda.

Truth be told, circa 2009 some of you generously gave our new progressive president partial credit for high (albeit misplaced) principles. Alas, the rose-colored glasses should have been put away years ago; your willingness to act as a good faith opponent has simply been "OBF" ("Overtaken by Facts").

Recall the significant number of experts who foresaw the suspicious fiscal projections accompanying the "Affordable Care Act," aka "Obamacare." Recall as well the aggressive defenses offered by the president and his acolytes—all so ready, willing, and able to impute the worst of motivations to those who saw through the negligently crafted, 2,700+-page monstrosity.

Now compare this Alinsky-ite *modus operandi* with WHAT WE KNOW NOW, i.e., the cynical manipulations contributed by Obamacare's chief architect—professor Jonathan Gruber. For those with short-term memory issues, recall these gratuitous quotations:

"This bill is written in a tortured way to ensure CBO did not score the mandate as taxes...if CBO scores the bill as taxes, it dies."

"Lack of transparency is a huge political advantage."

"Call it the stupidity of the American voter or whatever, but basically that was really, really critical for the thing to pass."

That these and related admissions embarrassed the administration (at least in the short term) is beyond question. Even Gruber attempted to walk back his words in the face of significant backlash, but to little avail. The damage was done; Obamacare was the law of the land. Deal with it.

Five years later, daily headlines bring constant reminders of what the not-so-honest professor and his enablers have brought: higher premiums and deductibles, fewer consumer options, significant insurer losses suffered on ACA exchanges, "The Little Sisters of the Poor" steamrolled by the federal government over an overreaching contraceptive mandate, more than half of Obamacare's nonprofit co-ops in bankruptcy, and drastically lower participation rates on exchange plans—far below budget analysts' projections.

Lack of transparency indeed.

Our next "truth be damned" episode concerns the anti-Mohammed video narrative supplied by the Obama administration in the aftermath of the Benghazi fiasco. Said storyline began with National Security Adviser Susan Rice's serial misrepresentations on five Sunday news shows:

> "What happened in Benghazi was in fact initially a spontaneous reaction to...the demonstrations against our facility in Cairo, which were prompted, of course, by the video."

Secretary of State Clinton's now infamous apology to the Muslim world for the video (that nobody saw) followed this misleading line. That Clinton thought it appropriate to convey the same talking points to the parents of slain American hero Ty Woods reflects the same Alinsky-ite tactic: Do whatever it takes to get over—just survive, because the (progressive) ends will always justify the political means.

Now fast-forward to a few weeks ago, and another bombshell from the Obama hierarchy, this time an admission from one of the president's closest advisers on the Iranian nuclear deal—a highly criticized agreement with the world's chief sponsor of terrorism.

The story's antagonist is national security "expert" (and author) Ben Rhodes—supposedly Mr. Obama's alter ego. It appears Rhodes invented a narrative regarding the alleged moderation of Iranian President Hassan Rouhani—solely in order to cover up Obama's early entreaties to the Iranian mullahs.

Here, such manipulation appears to be a source of great pride for Rhodes:

"The average reporter we talked to is 27 years old, and the only reporting experience consists of being around political campaigns.... They literally know nothing."

"[C]lueless reporters were saying things that validated what we [the administration] had given them to say."

And so a misleading narrative in support of a newly branded Iranian moderation was sold to friendly "force multipliers"—analysts from academia and the media—who were utilized anytime the media got close to the truth.

In this context, you might ask how many more times the Obama/Rhodes team can trot out the now so familiar mantra: "It's either *this* deal...OR THERE WILL BE WAR!" The answer appears to be forever—or at least until January 20, 2017—a date that can't arrive soon enough.

The final tallies on three vitally important policy initiatives from the Obama era:

Three thoroughly discredited narratives;

Three embarrassed Obama henchmen seeking to "clarify" their original statements; and

Three continuing disasters for the good ole USA.

My grandmother always told me "bad things come in threes." Now I believe her.

The Definition of Insanity

June 23, 2016, *Washington Examiner*

OK, it's going to be a brutal campaign. "The Donald" always plays for keeps, with the jugular as the usual target. On the other side, the Clintons are the proverbial roaches after a nuclear war—always surviving, even thriving, in the midst of chaos.

Yet, sooner or later, this unusual presidential election cycle will turn to issues—including *the* issue: Does America really want four more years of progressivism on steroids?

My purpose herein is not to analyze the familiar litany of Obama/Clinton offenses: Obamacare's myriad deficiencies, a sloppy and expensive stimulus, ultra-left Supreme Court nominees, big lies about the Iranian nuclear deal and Benghazi, a resurgent Islamic State in Iraq and Afghanistan, historically slow growth, major tax increases, and historic deficits.

Rather, this column is about what the pundits might label secondary issues—those that might not jump off the front page but nevertheless have serious impact on the state of our economy and culture.

Labor Policy

Continuously declining private-sector membership rolls are not a problem, as Big Labor calls the shots at Obama's Department of Labor. Despite a line of negative court decisions, this DOL has followed Labor's playbook on issues ranging from mandatory agency fees to higher minimum wages to union-dictated workplace organization.

Alas, few Washington special interests have done more to accelerate automation and eliminate entry-level jobs than those who claim to represent the "little guy." Such is life in today's Washington.

Israel

The animosity between Obama and Bibi Netanyahu was obvious from the start. But contrary to conventional Washington wisdom, such dysfunction was not damaging in the least to a progressive president demonstrating little regard for Israel's right-wing government.

Talk about having your cake and eating it too: Engage in regular browbeating of Mr. Netanyahu, allege massive growth in West Bank settlements (untrue), lend your political team to the Israeli opposition at election time, even downplay the strategic empowerment of the world's leading state sponsor of terror at Israel's doorstep, and still maintain majority political support among Jewish Americans.

I understand that the progressive appeal for younger, more secular Jews makes this policy turnabout easier, but few could have thought this move away from our strongest ally in the Middle East possible prior to Mr. Obama's presidency.

Today, it's not just possible—it's done. That the existential threat posed by Iran could be so successfully minimized is indeed quite a victory for Israel's numerous enemies.

Housing I

The old community organizer just won't give up. The infamous ACORN (now "Neighborhood Watch America") may be discredited, but leave it to the Obama Justice Department to find yet another way to shake down corporate America in the name of social justice.

Yes, you read that right: The Holder/Lynch DOJ negotiated the diversion of millions of dollars slated for casualties of the housing crisis to left-wing interest groups engaged in the usual "voter registration" and "mortgage counseling" efforts.

And, yes, "Neighborhood Watch America" is an extortion beneficiary of the banks' forced largesse. F.Y.I.: In some cases, it appears that every dollar "contributed" to a major settlement reduces the bank's debt by two dollars.

21

And so the same activists who cried "racism" when banks refused to underwrite subprime loans now receive diverted shakedown dollars from those same banks because the banks ended up underwriting the loans. What a country. And who said Eric Holder can't think outside the box?

Housing II

Many years ago, minorities who could otherwise afford more expensive suburban homes were "steered" away from certain white communities and zip codes. This practice was immoral and racist. The feds soon made it illegal as well with the passage of open housing laws.

But, typically, today's federal government is not satisfied with naturally occurring upward mobility. Today, Mr. Obama's HUD seeks to dictate the racial and ethnic makeup of America's suburbs. Neighborhoods tend to thrive when populated by people who can afford to live there regardless of race, ethnicity, or gender—a fact lost on Washington's all-knowing social engineers.

Speech

The proliferation of "speech codes" and "safe zones" on our college campuses is a national embarrassment. Yet, the coddling of our ultra-sensitive millennials proceeds apace. This tortured movement is nothing but a frontal attack on our First Amendment; you know, the one that the left used to celebrate.

Today, not so much, as illiberal progressives seek to limit speech that fails their ideological litmus test. Here is one remedy should Mr. Trump prevail in November: Tie loss of federal funds to the establishment of a speech-limited safe zone. Talk about a "trigger warning"—the loss of all those taxpayer dollars will surely depress our out-of-control college professors and administrators.

So if you have undecided friends, please remind them of the classic definition of insanity. In this case, four more years of this nonsense will leave us with an America we won't recognize—and not in a good way.

Read...and Repeat

July 21, 2016, *Washington Examiner*

Do you remember when the dynamic young U.S. Senator from Illinois assured us that the era of the "cowboy" Bush was over; that his pedigree as a Harvard Law grad and constitutional law professor would ensure a more palatable (and responsible) approach to the rule of law?

The last eight years paints quite a different picture. Indeed, the Obama tenure has witnessed ultra-aggressive rulemaking and extra-territorial executive orders in unprecedented number and scope. For context, check out my summaries of news headlines from the last seven-plus years. After reading, you may want to either reread *The Federalist Papers* or attend a Broadway production of *Hamilton*....

1. Supreme Court kills Obama administration's plan to defer deportation and provide work authorization for approximately four million illegal aliens;

2. Federal judge rules "cost-sharing" payments made to Obamacare insurers unconstitutional because authorization and appropriation by Congress are non-negotiable duties of the legislative branch;

3. Supreme Court orders Obama administration to compromise with "The Little Sisters of the Poor" over Obamacare's universal birth control mandate;

4. U.S. District Judge blocks Interior Department rule providing for stricter standards for hydraulic fracturing on public lands;

5. U.S. District Judge grants "limited discovery" into former Secretary of State Hillary Clinton's email matter, "even though it is exceedingly rare in FOIA cases";

6. Supreme Court suspends Obama administration's proposal to limit carbon emissions from power plants while legal challenges work their way through the courts;

7. U.S. District Judge reverses federal government's designation of insurer as a "systemically important" financial institution;

8. Supreme Court checks Obama's unprecedented attempt to expand recess appointment power by filling three vacancies in the National Labor Relations Board when Senate was still in session;

9. Eleven state attorneys general filed suit challenging the legality of the Obama Education Department's decision to require the nation's school districts to allow students to use bathrooms and locker rooms as a function of gender identity rather than biology; and

10. Federal judge rules in favor of House Republicans who had claimed the administration broke the law by paying Obamacare insurers without permission from Congress.

The breadth of Mr. Obama's overreach is historic and wholly compatible with Saul Alinsky's admonition that progressive ends must be reached by whatever means available (how else to achieve a transformative tenure?). Yet, these and many other media reports (I could fill the remainder of this column with similar bulletins) reveal that the judicial branch has stepped up to check many of Obama's most brazen power plays.

Ilya Shapiro, a senior fellow at Cato Institute, sums up Obama's relentless, yet mostly unsuccessful, regulatory power plays as follows:

"This term, the federal government argued an incredible ten cases without getting a single vote, not even that of one of President Obama's own nominees, Sonia Sotomayor and Elena Kagan. That brings his total to forty-four unanimous losses. For comparison, George W. Bush suffered thirty unanimous losses, while Bill Clinton withstood thirty-one. In other words, Barack Obama has lost unanimously 50 percent more often than his two immediate predecessors. These cases have been in such disparate areas as criminal procedure, religious liberty, property rights, immigration, securities regulation, tax law, and the separation of powers. The government's argument across this wide variety of cases [would have] essentially allowed the executive branch to do whatever it wants without meaningful constitutional restraint."

In the aftermath of FBI Director Comey's extraordinary oh-so-close non-referral regarding Hillary's private server fiasco, this is an important takeaway for disaffected conservatives otherwise ready to throw in the towel in the face of relentless Obama administrative edicts. Alas, the system (still) genuinely works. An independent judiciary still reigns. The administrative state still faces boundaries. Many of Obama's worst expansionary inclinations have been defeated or curtailed in the courts.

Of course, the optimism expressed herein will be wiped out should a third progressive administration come next January. Twelve years (maybe sixteen) of uber-left activist judges will likely complete the aforementioned transformation.

For those of you conservative types still not "feeling the Donald" and unable to fully appreciate the enormous stakes involved here, indulge me with a brief exercise: Review the Supreme Court voting records of Elena Kagan and Sonia Sotomayor. Then, research Judge Ruth Bader Ginsburg's recent tirade against candidate Trump. Then, reread this column. Then, come to your own conclusion.

Cleveland, Cockroaches, and the Clintons

August 4, 2016, *Washington Examiner*

1. You know it is going to be an unusual week at the Republican National Convention when your Uber driver greets you with, "Hi, I'm Muslim...and I'm big time for Donald Trump." The bottom line to our twenty-minute conversation: Trump is strong and will keep America safe while Hillary Clinton cannot be trusted to do the same.

2. Statistics don't lie: The economy is sleepwalking its way to the weakest recovery since 1949. And slow growth is the fuel that has powered the populist ascendancies of Donald Trump and Bernie Sanders. All of which puts Clinton in a box: Run as Obama's third term and thereby ignore his weak economic record, or indict the slow recovery and risk turning off an Obama-loving Democratic base.

3. The irony of a New York City real estate mogul connecting with working-class voters in Rust Belt states is not lost on those of us who campaigned with Mitt Romney through coal country four years ago. Romney, the successful businessman, marketed a Trump-like message—"I'll be the country's CEO"—but failed to close the deal with enough of these targeted households to flip Ohio, Michigan, Pennsylvania, or Wisconsin. Not so with Trump this cycle. Perhaps another four years of abysmal growth has gained the attention of this vital block, most of whom do not resent wealth or the one percent.

4. Seems everyone is talking about Pennsylvania—and for good reason. Many GOP pundits consider it to be the most "flippable" of states on Trump's narrow path to the presidency. The calculus is not complicated: Clinton must maximize African American turnout in Philadelphia to maintain a Democratic

winning streak dating back to 1992. Conversely, Trump must be competitive with white women in the Philadelphia suburbs. Remember, the "Keystone State" trends red during off-cycle elections (Republicans control both chambers of the legislature) when base Democrats tend to go missing.

5. Athletic coaches stress that mere activity is different from production. The former marks time, the latter propels one to a goal. Likewise, political campaigns market a candidate's résumé—as opposed to a candidate's successes (progress). Keep this distinction in mind while pondering Clinton's reminder that she visited 112 countries while Secretary of State. Now ask yourself how many of these visits produced a positive outcome for the United States.

   Russia? Nope, the vaunted reset of bilateral relations has been a disaster. China? Just increased tension and more showdowns in the South China Sea. Libya? What about all those pleas for additional security at our consulate in Benghazi? Israel? Recall it was her administration that dispatched a political hit team to defeat Benjamin Netanyahu two years ago. Saudi Arabia, Jordan, Egypt, the United Arab Emirates? These Sunni Muslim allies fear our new friendship with the world's most aggressive state sponsor of terror (Iran); their recent overtures to Putin speak volumes about how they feel about Obama/Clinton-era foreign policy.

   Of course, just showing up 112 times is appealing to some because...it shows you care. But such naiveté is dangerous. Hopefully, we are not too far from the day our enemies (again) fear us and our allies (again) respect us.

6. Speaking of the Democratic nominee, many of my GOP friends remain fatalistic when it comes to her political survival. FBI Director James Comey's non-indictment indictment of Clinton was only the latest chapter in that well-known book, *The Only Things to Survive a Nuclear Attack Will Be Cockroaches*

and the Clintons. The litany of Hillary's near-death experiences is impressive: Travelgate, Cattlefuturegate, Whitewater, Rose Law Firm billing records, Hillarycare, Vince Foster, Monica Lewinsky, Norman Hsu, bimbo eruptions, sniper fire scandal, Benghazi, Emailgate, and the Clinton Foundation—among others.

But such cynicism must be weighed against present reality: Clinton is unpopular. More than 50 percent of Americans view her unfavorably; two-thirds of us believe she doesn't tell the truth. Of course, my buddies would be justified in their cynicism if Clinton survives to win the presidency. But don't count your chickens just yet: Three decades of scandal does tend to stain a politician's image, and even Clinton is no exception.

7. One of the more tangible scandals this cycle is the ongoing mess at the Department of Veterans Affairs. This agency is tasked with one duty: Take care of the people who fought and were injured in the defense of our freedom. Long waiting lists that led to premature, inexcusable deaths and suicides made this a sensational (if not horrific) saga when the story initially broke. Lately, we learn of millions of dollars in expensive artwork at VA facilities and an explosion of non-physician hiring. But thanks to groups such as OpenTheBooks.com, taxpayers have more tools to hold this wildly inefficient agency accountable. Here, Trump is right on with a plan to revitalize a broken system. The mistreatment of injured vets is immoral and should never be tolerated.

Going Forward

September 15, 2016, *Washington Examiner*

The Obama experiment in uber-progressivism has constricted labor participation, doubled our national debt, postponed our entitlement crisis, degraded sovereignty, damaged race relations, and emboldened our enemies.

For the GOP, the primary season witnessed all stripes of conservatives offering up varying (mostly) conservative strategies for what ails us. Yet, the people chose the anti-PC, anti-establishment billionaire who spoke to the country's struggling, angry working class.

On the Democratic side, Hillary Clinton has doubled down on identity politics, higher taxes, greater regulation, sanctuary cities, climate protocols, an ever-increasing minimum wage, and further disengagement from world hot spots.

Now, alas, Labor Day has come and gone—and the final campaign push has begun. All of which calls for a sober list of items that move the country away from collectivism and toward a post-progressive future.

Grow the Economy

The Democrats' domestic agenda (minimum wage, living wage, gender-pay equity, protectionism, CEO pay cap, etc.) is directly from the Occupy playbook. We know two things about such economic populism: 1) It sounds really good when you say it real fast; and 2) It contains lousy prescriptions for economic growth. A reminder: Progressives believe market economics to be a "zero-sum" game. That is, some become poor because others become rich, and vice versa.

In response, the GOP must return to its Reagan-Kemp "opportunity society" roots that stresses lifting all boats—not simply the ones government-sponsored crony capitalists choose to rescue. Real growth cures many ills—especially the specter of twenty-six-year-olds living in their parents' basements.

Reform the Tax Code

Our brief 1990s infatuation with the flat tax should remind us that comprehensive reform will be a hazardous duty. That love affair ended unceremoniously when Middle America figured out its favorite preferences were on the chopping block. Home mortgage deduction? But my wife is a Realtor. Charitable deduction? But we have so many wonderful nonprofits in our state! Accelerated depreciation? But how do we rebuild American manufacturing? It took a true-believing, two-term, popular president and plenty of bipartisan support to pass comprehensive reform in 1986—but only after almost a decade of policy debate.

Nevertheless, long-term prosperity will be boosted by fewer brackets, fewer preferences, a capital gains rate that rewards capital formation—and the drastic lowering of the world's highest corporate income tax.

Reform Entitlements

"W" tried (and failed) to use his post-9/11 credibility to pass private Social Security accounts. A few years later, Paul Ryan offered a bipartisan Medicare reform that became the focus of Democratic attack ads around the country. Today, the mere mention of entitlement reform sends progressives into fits of class warfare frenzy.

Nevertheless, the numbers are staggering. A soon-to-be $20 trillion federal debt. Mandatory spending that eats up 70 percent of federal outlays. And out-of-control Medicaid spending that drives unsustainable state budget deficits.

Can a responsible reform package be non-suicidal? Answer: Maybe, especially if this "Trumpian" era means voters are willing to listen to uncomfortable facts and substantive fixes. A start would be a new, phased-in retirement age of seventy. Means testing of Medicare and Social Security benefits would attract bipartisan support. And so would allowing beneficiaries who work beyond retirement age to keep more after-tax income as long as they do not claim benefits.

Reassert American Leadership

We now know why President Bush 41 allowed Saddam Hussein to survive at the end of Desert Storm. In the Middle East, it seems the removal of even murderous thugs can lead to unforeseen, violent results.

But it is not America's ill-fated exercise in Iraqi regime change alone that has further destabilized a persistently unstable region. A failed "Arab Spring," unrelenting Shia-Sunni conflicts, and the emergence of a brutal Islamic "caliphate" guarantee continued instability.

Aligned against this dangerous environment has been an Obama administration intent on 1) inaction or 2) negligible action. Here, an anti-war president's favorite narrative is never far removed from the national debate: "America either retreats—disengages, leaves, signs weak agreements—or THERE WILL BE WAR." Vladimir Putin, Bashar Assad, and Sayyid Ali Khamenei are happy to leverage this Obama doctrine.

The GOP must stress the importance of negotiating from positions of strength rather than consistently rewarding those who seek to humiliate us. Recall Churchill's admonition from an earlier, equally dangerous era: "An appeaser is one who feeds the crocodile hoping it will eat him last."

What to do? We must establish a Syrian no-fly zone, offer arms and intel support to Syrian moderates, relentlessly bomb the Islamic State (there has been some recent progress), and re-energize our alliance with our Sunni allies. Two further planks: No more public commitments wherein the U.S. military telegraphs its intent to leave the battleground on a specific timetable. And no more embarrassing attempts at moral equivalency; America is not perfect, but our little experiment in pluralism and freedom is really exceptional (Barack Obama's protestations to the contrary notwithstanding).

Rewrite Obamacare

Fortunately, a number of the statute's most problematic provisions will be easy to fix, including repeal of the hated medical device tax, the employer mandate and the individual mandate, as well as a new and not-so-improved conscience clause (the well-established policy that religious institutions are not required to provide health services that violate their religious convictions that the Supreme Court has now ordered modified). Also beyond repair are Obamacare's co-ops, a majority of which are bankrupt. Similarly, the high deductible, pricey, one-size-fits-all exchange options are proving to be unattractive and will surely follow the same failed path—more quickly if Congress continues to cut off taxpayer subsidies.

A rewritten statute will increase competition and consumer choice. A market-oriented approach would bless interstate underwriting and the growth of individually owned medical savings accounts.

Regarding Medicaid, those states that have expanded their rolls in order to gain access to additional federal matching dollars should be allowed the option to "devolve"—a paradigm that would empower more efficient state health departments to call the shots for a program originally targeted to poor women with children.

Immigration

Open borders, driver's license privileges, voting privileges, in-state college tuition, welfare benefits, and sanctuary cities have generated divisive debate over the last two decades.

Conservatives demand sovereignty, assimilation, and the rule of law. Progressives, not so much. Indeed, progressive politicians at all levels continue to defend a dangerous ad hoc respect for the law—and a seeming disregard for border security.

A majority of Americans want border enforcement and a legal process that welcomes all who desire to assimilate, learn English, follow the law, respect pluralism and religious freedom, and love their new country.

A bill that incorporates these features will close an ugly chapter in an otherwise wonderful story of a wildly successful immigrant nation.

Rewrite Dodd-Frank

A bipartisan drive toward affordable housing goals was the fundamental driver of the mortgage-induced recession—a fact of life wholly irrelevant to the community organizer in the White House. It was equally irrelevant to the drafters of Dodd-Frank. Their focus was corporate greed and "Too Big to Fail" Wall Street investment banks (the same ones the federal government begged for help during the crisis) that sold toxic mortgage packages to the world, consequences be damned.

Today, a variety of economic repercussions are apparent: higher bank fees, less liquidity, tighter credit, and a blizzard of paperwork. Fewer small banks and increased federal control over the lending marketplace is not a prescription for economic recovery, or growth.

The administration's recent attempts to revisit weaker underwriting standards while maintaining taxpayer guarantees against losses should be repealed on the new president's first day. "All good intentions" does not a housing policy make; it is not "compassionate" to give people mortgages they cannot afford.

Pass an Urban New Deal

The "Great Society" underclass is now 50 years, 80 federal agencies, and 23 trillion dollars down the road—without much to brag about. The unemployment rate for the bottom 20 percent is *over* 20 percent, and labor participation is at its lowest point since the Carter administration. Seems it is indeed impossible to fight a successful "war" from the corner of 17th and K Street, NW.

From the jump, the Democrats have championed big, centralized government agencies—and have stuck to the program despite decades of demonstrable dysfunction. Alas, big government proponents never seem to grasp that more regulation means more dependence.

Everyone has their own ideas, but surely program consolidation (Paul Ryan has done good work here) and the devolving of authority (read: money) back to the states is a commonsense starting point. Governors and local officials know best what works in their local communities.

Other worthy elements are increasing the "Earned Income Tax Credit," radical school choice (yes, I mean vouchers where schools are serial failures), and radical property tax reform (the first step toward attracting private employers back to the city). More involved fathers (see below) is a mandatory addition.

Revisit Paris

The recently concluded world climate change talks in Paris saw the president volunteer an American CO_2 emissions target (26 to 28 percent from 2005 levels) and a compliance year (2025) to the "historic agreement" before declaring victory and jetting off in his fossil fuel–guzzling super jet.

Media reports of the agreement tended to either minimize or ignore the randomness of the (reduction) targets, the myriad admission sources covered by the goals, and the issue of how any president (lacking legal authority) could force said sources into compliance.

A Republican alternative would include wind, solar, and biofuels—where generated economically and rationally (i.e., without crony capitalism–inspired taxpayer money) AND a continuing push for a natural gas revolution that has done much to propel America toward real energy independence.

Champion Fatherhood

It has been fifty years since Daniel Patrick Moynihan warned that the African American family was in rapid decline. Alas, Moynihan's analysis was limited; the last five decades have witnessed a similar decline in the white and brown family structures. And both of these unsettling developments come with an unsurprising common denominator: more children raised without fathers than ever before.

The results are irrefutable. Children in father-absent homes are:

- Four times more likely to be poor
- At dramatically greater risk of drug and alcohol abuse
- More than twice as likely to commit suicide
- Show higher levels of aggressive behavior than children born to married mothers

A half century of analysis reveals what most of us would otherwise suspect: Federal welfare programs contribute to the rise of single-parent homes. But this problem is not merely the result of failed policy measures. It is cultural as well.

All of us know of single parents who have worked hard and achieved remarkable results in raising their children. America appropriately applauds such efforts. Yet it is not disrespectful to remind Americans that more often than not such family structures constitute a direct ticket to poverty—and broken children. The best way out of poverty is a two-income household.

And One More

Barack Hussein Obama's judicial appointments daily inflict damage in ways seldom noticeable or understood by the average citizen. Accordingly, they infuse leftist construction on the most divisive issues of the day: voter photo identification, affirmative action, immigration enforcement, religious freedom, gun rights, mandatory union fees, and school choice, to name a few.

This daily carnage pales in comparison to what a new Democratic president could do with a likely three new Supreme Court appointments. For context, check out the voting records of Justices Elena Kagan and Sonia Sotomayor. Then get to work organizing your precinct. The stakes have never been higher.

What the Washington Establishment Never Understood

November 11, 2016, *Washington Examiner*

The "Secret Trump voter phenomenon" did indeed exist. I had dismissed such a theory earlier in the campaign but observed too many examples of it in real time. This subtle behavior was notably present among millennial Trump supporters who chose to mind their Ps and Qs in the face of *overwhelming* disapproval from their peers.

Speaking of which, my numerous appearances on college campuses brought home what polls have shown: The millennial generation is more progressive than previous iterations of left-leaning young people. A "tolerance mantra" prevails here—most especially reflected in persistently permissive views on social issues. Interestingly, however, my aggressive condemnation of the academic anti-speech movement ("speech codes," "trigger warnings," "safe zones," etc.) was not met with the expected strong opposition. Most of the vitriol on campus was reserved for Donald Trump. Most-asked question: "What would Mr. Trump have to do for *you* to retract *your* endorsement?"

The tone and tenor of campaign 2016 changed dramatically over the last two weeks—and not simply due to James Comey's renewed look at Hillary Clinton's email trail. It was more of an unexpected Trump discipline that took hold on the stump. Gone were the gratuitous tweets and extemporaneous asides that had frequently landed him in hot water. The new Trump stuck to substance (Obamacare, immigration, taxes) with little more than a scripted shot or two at Clinton's continuing ethics problems.

Despite considerable analysis devoted to the unique nature of this campaign season, the philosophical divide on the major issues of the day came down to...quite traditional lines. Clinton versus Trump was about the progressive Democrat versus the (mostly) conservative Republican. Here, under no circumstances would the aggressively progressive Clinton be confused with her "the era of big government is over" husband; credit for this left-hand turn must be given to the newly dominant Warren/Sanders wing of the party. As for Trump, the last days were devoted to tax reform, immigration reform (ending sanctuary cities), law and order, trade policy, and a promise to repeal the rapidly disintegrating Obamacare monster—all predictable positions straight out of the GOP playbook.

Trump's win can be attributed in large part to the efforts of Kellyanne Conway. An undisputed dumpster fire of a campaign was transformed beginning with her ascension to campaign manager on August 17. Notwithstanding a few episodes of unplanned, middle-of-the-night tweets and successful Clinton attempts to bait him during debates, the post-Kellyanne Trump could stick to a prepared script and even stay on message when straying from his teleprompter. That she was able to stop her candidate's preference for late-night one-on-one cable interviews is a testament to her sway over a man who not so long ago reveled in his independence from the professional consultant class.

In the end, Bernie Sanders proved to be more loyal Democrat than revolutionary troublemaker. Recall the numerous (WikiLeaks and other) revelations wherein it was revealed how Debbie Wasserman Schultz and others within the Washington Democratic establishment sought to degrade the upstart challenger from Vermont. Talk about "rigged"! Yet, Sanders proved a reliable campaign surrogate for Clinton. My college appearances only served to underline his popularity on campus as liberal college kids ate up his anti-establishment, income inequality message.

This election was all about domestic issues and scandals—not so much strategies in the War on Terror or America's place in the world going forward. All of which supports the old axiom that economic uncertainty focuses everyone's mind...on the homefront.

What better pre-election night metaphor for Donald Trump than the likes of Bon Jovi, Miley Cyrus, Katy Perry, and Beyoncé (and many other Hollywood types) shilling for Hillary while the Trump

Train was drawing huge crowds barnstorming throughout the Rust Belt.

The Washington establishment never did grasp the economic angst of flyover America's working class. The median income for working-class Americans is lower today than it was in 1999. The resulting frustration was reflected in Trump wins in Ohio, Wisconsin, Michigan, and Pennsylvania.

Facts and Opinions

November 24, 2016, *Washington Examiner*

Do not buy the "America is (now) a racist country" indictment against Trump. About a third of the subdivisions Obama carried in 2012 went for Trump. And there have been no reports of a sudden influx of Klan members into these districts over the last four years. Rather, these were/are classic swing voters disillusioned with Obama-era slow growth and attracted to Trump's anti-establishment messaging.

Obamacare proved to be the gift that keeps on giving.

The latest Obamacare rate hikes hit the market days prior to the election. It is estimated that 33 states will have fewer insurance carriers in 2017 than 2016, and 20 percent of consumers will be left with only one carrier serving their local market. Fact: Democrats have lost 63 House seats, 9 Senate seats, 13 governorships, 524 state legislative seats, and 18 State Chambers since the terribly misnamed "Affordable Care Act" was foisted on the American people without a single vote from the minority party. Per Nancy Pelosi, I guess the people really did find out what was "in it."

Changing demographics were not enough to deliver Clinton from white working-class dissatisfaction with the Obama economic record.

Trump won the white vote by a record margin of 58/47 percent despite whites dropping from 72 to 70 percent of the total electorate. Yet long-term trend lines clearly favor Democrats given the party's proven appeal to America's minority communities. Nevertheless, Democrats' preoccupation with identity politics and victimization narratives is a guaranteed turn-off for a vast white working class frustrated with its economic (mis)fortunes and a progressive political correctness culture out of step with great swaths of flyover America.

Middle America: 1 / Establishment Elitists: 0

The hangdog looks on the faces of the cable news outlets not named Fox reflected all you needed to know about media establishment attitudes. This well-educated elite could not/would not bring itself to acknowledge the widespread angst, distrust, and unrest among those who do not read *The New York Times* or *Washington Post*. But the numbers say it all: Trump won white voters without college degrees by a stunning 67/28 margin. Trump won white evangelical Christians (includes Protestants, Catholics, Mormons, and others) by 81/16 percent. And Trump almost split union households with Clinton. The bottom line: Most of the people who work with their hands, attend religious services, and do not begrudge wealth or success simply reject the progressives' agenda of "free stuff" and grievance politics. Whether the Democratic Party will moderate its platform or double down on Warren/Sanders liberalism remains to be seen. (I'll take the "under.")

Huge black turnout remains essential to Democratic success.

Clinton beat Trump 88/8 among African Americans, but black turnout was down 8 percent from 2012 (despite the Herculean efforts of the Democratic turnout machine in America's major cities), all of which spelled the difference between defeat and victory in the critical states of Michigan and Pennsylvania. Here, Bill Clinton's enduring positive image with African American voters (recall "the First Black President") did not translate to his wife.

The gender gap was not much different than four years ago.

Trump lost among all female voters by 12 points—54/42, representing only a one-point drop-off from 2012. Trump won white women by a margin of 53/43 and white married women by approximately 20 points—a predictable result from this usually solid red constituency.

Among Hispanic voters, a Cuban plurality remains solid GOP.

The Obama administration's liberalization of ties with Cuba was supposed to spark youthful Democrat enthusiasm among this key voter bloc in Florida. Yet, Trump carried the Florida-based Cuban community 54/41 (compared to Clinton's overwhelming 71/26 advantage among non-Cuban Latinos). Seems that Raúl's doubling down on domestic oppression in the aftermath of President Obama's well-documented opening did not give Florida Democrats much to crow about.

From the irony department.

A few days after the election, I watched a national cable show wherein a leading House Democrat talked about his party's goal of recapturing the recently discovered white working class. He then proceeded to endorse numerous Democratic mayors who are promising to resist Trump's plan to round up and deport *criminal illegal aliens*. Parenthetical question: Doesn't every twelve-step program require one to admit they have a problem before beginning to fix it?

Here We Go Again

December 23, 2016, *Washington Examiner*

We have seen this movie before.

Recall Bush-Gore, circa 2000. A razor-thin margin in Florida, the emergence of "hanging chads," a popular vote win for the challenger, relentless media coverage, and claims of voter intimidation and fraud.

Repercussions began shortly after the final ballot was cast, including claims of a "stolen" election. Predictably, there was outrage from leaders of the civil rights industry. (You might recall that cycle's NAACP-sponsored television ad wherein George W. Bush was associated with the murder of James Byrd because he had failed to support a "hate crimes" bill in Texas.)

The political environment turned ugly. No WMD was found in Iraq. A "Bush lied—people died" narrative was produced—including from members of Congress who had seen the pre-war intelligence and voted *for* the war. The rhetoric proved quite successful in degrading George W. Bush and delegitimizing the Bush presidency in the minds of some. It also paved the way for the anti-war Barack Obama to win the presidency.

Yet, all this seems like child's play compared to the shenanigans that have followed the results of November 8, 2016.

Indeed, it is difficult to imagine a more relentless character assault than the one we have witnessed since that historic day. (It has certainly placed the GOP establishment's early, rather feeble campaign to degrade Trump and his movement in clearer perspective.)

The Democrats' delegitimization campaign began in earnest once Trump emerged as a serious contender for the GOP nomination. The central premise: "unfit" for high public office. Remarkably, Hillary Clinton thought to openly degrade her opponent's supporters ("a basket of deplorables"). When Trump said he might not recognize the results of a "rigged" election—well, the "unfit" indictment went full tilt.

Then came election night. Inaccurate exit polls were the first sign of trouble. Next, the "Blue Wall" began to crumble in Wisconsin. Said crumbling was followed by forlorn looks of disbelief from cable anchors not employed by Fox. Reality took a particularly ugly turn when Rust Belt districts that had twice voted for Obama came in "Trump." This somehow was interpreted as latent racism—as though there had been a large secret migration of Klan supporters to the Midwest over the past four years.

It all came crashing down on November 9. Street protests in major American cities. "Snowflake" college students demanding "cry-ins," coloring books, therapy dogs, and expanded "safe zones." And who can forget Miley Cyrus with her tearful video to the world...followed by a chorus of whiny Hollywood types who always promise to leave the country, but never actually do.

A new twist this time around were calls to end the Electoral College. The Democrats have won six of the last seven popular votes for president. Long-term racial and ethnic trend lines favor them. Accordingly, party leaders now advocate for a popular vote format—all in order to stop those Republican rednecks in flyover America from pulling one out every now and then. Per this revisionist view, any president taking office after losing the popular vote is by definition "illegitimate."

And so it was no big surprise that a coalition of former Clinton supporters and a true-believing contingent from the Green Party would attempt to fund recounts in key battleground states.

But this chapter in progressive revisionism was cut short when Russian hacking of DNC emails came to light. Now, the left temporarily rediscovered the merits of the EC—and those electors who are *not* constitutionally mandated to vote according to the results of the popular vote in their states.

This storyline being that anyone who has had something positive to say about Vladimir Putin or Russia during a cycle wherein Russian operatives attempted to hack Democratic *and* Republican emails is "unfit" to be president.

Alas, this effort too was doomed from the beginning. The complainants did not produce one shred of evidence that Russian hacking impacted the actual vote. In fact, quite to the contrary, according to the forty-forth president of the United States. Still, another week or so of "unfit for office" indictments were thrown around for public consumption. Do not think for a second such a narrative will waste away in light of this week's Electoral College vote.

Rather, we have just witnessed the beginning of what promises to be a relentless four-year campaign to delegitimize all things Trump—by whatever means available. A similar movie played to rave reviews on the left during the first years of the new millennium. It is what America's progressive party seems to do best these days.

Hard to Leave

January 5, 2017, *Washington Examiner*

There is a budding enthusiasm in flyover America these days.

Its foundation is a growing belief that America's economic might will soon be rekindled by a businessman-president. The initial macro-economic signs are promising. Consumer confidence is up. And a Trump-inspired Wall Street rally has the Dow at record heights.

The construction of the Trump cabinet has been another breath of fresh air. This group is heavy on relevant experience, private-sector success, and conservative values. It is also quite wealthy. Accordingly, mainstream media coverage has been generally hostile. No surprise there. Its agenda of high taxes, high regulation, high preemption, high political correctness, and *getting* high (marijuana legalization) is now on ice. These disconsolate pundits understand their time in the wilderness has arrived.

Yet, President Obama's final days have served to remind those of us who have been walking around with a smile for the last two months that he remains the contemptuous ultra-left progressive we have so adamantly opposed over the past eight years.

Some of you have been preoccupied with more pleasant tasks such as the Christmas holidays or the lead-up to the National Football League playoffs. If so, the following bulletins will serve as an ice bucket over the head of cold reality:

- Obama's six-year ballot-box losing streak has not diminished his passion for federal preemption in the least. Accordingly, the soon-to-be-dismissed lefties at the White House and its executive agencies have been working overtime to shove as many new rules down America's throat as humanly possible.

Some of the major initiatives (shutting down pipelines, a new "permanent" drilling ban in the Arctic and Atlantic Oceans, and new

45

limits on coal exploration) have garnered headlines—many others have not. Here's hoping the new Trump administration will follow its instincts and reject much of this stealthy last-minute rulemaking. We should expect similar close scrutiny of the 250 executive orders, 230 "executive memoranda," and an unknown number of informal "guidance letters" issued by Obama regulators. A pro-growth Congress stands ready to assist, as does a job creation class anxiously awaiting the installation of a president who has signed the *front* of payroll checks.

- The relentless assault on all things Bibi Netanyahu and the State of Israel took one final duplicitous twist with the historic U.S. decision to "abstain" from a United Nations resolution harshly critical of settlement activity in the Palestinian territories. Worse, a number of top Israeli officials believe the Obama administration orchestrated the resolution. U.S. vetoes over the past thirty-six years had killed similar initiatives, but the man who had unsuccessfully attempted to defeat Netanyahu during his re-election campaign of 2015, and who no longer has to appease Jewish voters, could not pass up one last opportunity to weaken the State of Israel before his favorite anti-American world body. Leftist Israeli haters applauded the treachery. U.S. abandonment of the Jewish state is their goal, but (much) happier times await.

Trump's election may have generated real consternation in capitals around the world, but not in Israel. No world leader will be happier to see President-elect Trump replace Obama than Bibi Netanyahu.

- Who can forget candidate Obama's relentless campaign assaults on our Guantanamo Bay prison facility? The specialty prison was repeatedly cited as a primary reason our enemies hate us so much. The importance of the issue led Obama to sign an executive order mandating the facility's closure on day two of his new administration!

Now fast-forward to today. Obama may be in the home stretch, but expedited departures from Gitmo are clearly on the menu. Only 64 terror detainees remain from the 242 housed at the island fortress when Obama took over. And it now appears the president will release up to 19 additional terrorists to Italy, Oman, Saudi Arabia, and the United Arab Emirates before leaving office.

Obama, Biden, and Kerry have expended plenty of energy in attempting to keep Obama's original promise. Nevertheless, it now appears a residual population of around forty will "greet" President-elect Trump.

Intensive tracking by the non-partisan Office of the Director of National Intelligence projects that approximately one-third of the detainees freed under Presidents Bush and Obama are confirmed or believed to have returned to jihad. A not-so-politically-correct Trump administration understands the stakes. The expedited releases need to stop. The American public does not view these terror soldiers as common street criminals. A majority does not want terror soldiers housed in our federal penitentiaries. Gitmo must remain open for the worst-of-the-worst enemy combatants.

- The outgoing anti-fossil fuel ideologue in the White House has not been a happy camper. The world is awash in cheap oil, and sales of gas-guzzling sport utility vehicles are through the roof. What to do? Well, why not add to your world record of designating western venues as "national monuments" in order to cordon them off from energy development? This deed was accomplished in the post-Christmas announcement wherein an additional 1.6 million acres of southwestern Utah and southern Nevada was declared off limits.

Note that no president has ever revoked a predecessor's monument designation. Note, also, that one Donald J. Trump does not appear captive to such precedence.

Restoring Freedom to America's Cultural Menu

January 19, 2017, *Washington Examiner*

The Obama era is done. A peaceful transition of power has taken place. As the kids say, "all good." Okay, maybe not *all* good. This time, it's a bit more complicated. This time, the country walked back "hope and change" and chose instead broken eggs and hurt feelings. In blue America, continuing angst will surely follow.

But interwoven with the daily, often ugly conflict is plenty of happy news for America's deplorables. You know, those of us who prefer Vince Vaughan to Meryl Streep—and Zac Brown to Bon Jovi.

A sampling from the red side:

Jobs

Carrier, Ford, Fiat, Chrysler, and Amazon have issued releases proclaiming major job retention/expansion plans, while the financial press is full of stories about increasing business confidence and an expected capital expenditures boom. The specific reasons for the uplifting announcements vary across business sectors, but a common denominator is impossible to miss: a new president who believes "You built that." President-elect Trump's vast experience in building his own "that" bolsters the notion he has the backs of America's job creators. What a refreshing change from Mr. Obama's worn-out class warfare.

Right-to-Work

Not so long ago, a Wisconsin or Michigan right-to-work law was a pipe dream. Today, it is *the* law in both states. In fact, RTW is now the law in twenty-seven states, with Missouri and New Hampshire likely soon to join the stampede. A new iteration in states with union-dominated legislatures is the so-called "local option," which allows individual subdivisions to opt in. Initial court challenges to the local option have been unsuccessful.

School Choice

Few issues get progressive hearts fluttering faster than school choice. Add a voucher component and you have complete meltdown. Such explains the emotional reaction to Betsy DeVos, a leading charter school advocate and Trump's choice to be Secretary of Education.

History is not on the unions' side. Choice means opportunity for many poor parents with kids stuck in underperforming schools. These same parents regularly line up to secure prized slots in charter school lotteries in our most poverty-stricken neighborhoods. And no amount of opposition from the civil rights industry can stop the momentum. Coming next: a Trump-inspired federally funded voucher initiative. You can bet the fight will be nasty.

Political Correctness

That the most anti-politically correct candidate in modern history could win 306 electoral votes represents a serious rejection of the progressive narrative. And so it is now socially acceptable to recognize that "hands up, don't shoot" did *not*, in fact, occur; that there is a wide gulf between "ethnic profiling" and "criminal profiling" (former fed Rudy Giuliani did *not* target Irish social clubs when going after the Mafia); that protected class interests do not trump religious freedom in every setting; that a country without borders cannot long function as a sovereign; and that "Merry Christmas" is (still) a constitutionally acceptable option when greeting a fellow human being in December.

Moreover, the political indoctrination that passes for instruction on so many of our college campuses is now receiving more analysis—and rebuke. Thanks (in part) goes to the thousands of wannabe community activists who have assumed the role of college administrator/professor in order to influence impressionable young minds. Their well-publicized "cry-ins," "sympathy cookies," and post-election "safe zones" revealed an intellectual immaturity and naiveté that garnered national headlines. And to think that their great-grand-parents sacrificed everything to fight and win the Second World War—without *one* safe zone!

The Media

Antagonism between the "mainstream" media and GOP presidents is not new. But today's media paradigm is unique. Policy by daily tweet is certainly new, as is an unbridled willingness to engage hostile media face-to-face. The new president cares a great deal about the substance of media reports—but has little use for media "feelings." In other words, he will always respond to opinion masquerading as news, or what he deems to be "fake news." That his task is often accomplished through incendiary language speaks to the latter. My man-on-the-street quick polls tell me that such vitriol directed toward hostile media types is a big hit—at least in the short term. Suffice it to say that for the next four years our "friends" in the progressive media should prepare for repeated altercations. DJT would have it no other way.

Supreme Court

Despite a barrage of criticism, Mitch McConnell and a GOP Senate majority did not allow Mr. Obama to fill Justice Scalia's prized seat. A GOP president and Senate will now ensure a conservative major-ity on the court and also fill the more than one hundred vacancies in the federal circuits. These new judges will not view the judiciary as a super legislature to be engaged in the business of social engineering. This is a very big deal—and a very good result for a country and cul-ture placed at risk by eight years of activist appointees.

Obama's progressive era lasted eight years. An uncomfortable mix of class warfare, identity politics, federal preemption, and lead-ing from behind proved plenty unpopular outside of faculty lounges, sanctuary cities, and the alphabet soup of cable news networks. The new administration seems poised to restore freedom to America's cul-ture menu. All good...

CHAPTER 2

Trump Unplugged: A New Era Begins

One line from the forty-fifth president's inaugural address spoke volumes to a divided nation: *"We are transferring power from Washington, DC, and giving it back to you, the people."*

What better message could be delivered to millions of alienated working-class laborers and small business owners turned on by Trump's highly touted résumé and can-do attitude? And what more discouraging thought could be heard by blue America, most of whose members had spent the previous eight years celebrating the arrival of a supercharged social permissiveness and empowered federal government?

And so a new era of Trump-style populism (with a healthy side dose of nationalism) began. One of the new president's first acts was to exit the Obama-negotiated Trans-Pacific Partnership (TPP). Other first-week executive orders and instructions included imposition of a federal hiring freeze, the initial procedural steps toward Obamacare repeal, a Keystone Pipeline revival, construction of a southern border wall, a pause on legal immigration from seven countries with a history of terrorist activities, and a Pentagon-directed order to formulate a battle plan to defeat ISIS—deliverable within thirty days.

Few close observers could feign surprise. These initial actions sought to fulfill a number of Trump's most prominent campaign promises. They were also mostly consistent with his prior (pre-politics) interviews and speeches. But the man and the message were met with deep and abiding opposition from members of the loyal opposition and fourth estate, beginning from the very moment stunned television anchors announced his unlikely victory. Indeed, the tears from Mrs. Clinton's long-scheduled New York City victory party had barely subsided when the progressive opposition began to reboot for the long fight. Initial reaction focused on the improbable lobbying of the appointed members of the Electoral College to switch their votes during the tally of electors. The failure of this Hollywood-inspired vote switching campaign led to calls for ending the Electoral College itself— a topic that dominated anti-Trump cable news networks for weeks.

Unsurprisingly, race was raised as another disqualifying factor. On election night, progressive pundit Van Jones labeled the election a "whitelash," an indictment of white working-class voters who had turned out for Trump in overwhelming numbers. The remark reflected widespread progressive outrage at Trump's victory but lost context when analysts reminded viewers that many of these same voters had supported Barack Obama in the preceding two elections!

In a similar vein, civil rights icon Representative John Lewis of Georgia led approximately sixty Democrats in what amounted to a boycott of the inaugural address. Lewis initially claimed it would be the first inaugural he would miss. Left-leaning news outlets gushed. Rep. Lewis was now the leader of a new resistance—until media reports surfaced that he had pulled the *same* stunt at George W. Bush's festivities. He must have simply forgotten. Still, the Lewis-led protest injected race back into Washington's (un)welcome wagon for Mr. Trump.

The post-election angst came together in anti-Trump woman-power rallies held around the country. The primary vehicle was a "women's march" on Washington that drew an estimated 500,000. (Predictably, a feminist, pro-life women's group was removed from the list of parade sponsors—this iteration of woman power brought its very own litmus test to the proceedings.) It was here that Madonna uttered her infamous line: "I have thought an awful lot about blowing up the White House." Precious few deep thoughts were heard during the course of the proceedings.

The rallies may have had the "women" moniker, but opposition to everything Trump was the primary focus for Congressional Democrats acting as foot soldiers for the resistance. The public relations portion of the effort was duly accomplished with the help of a sympathetic media.

Shortly thereafter, rank-and-file Democrats happily doubled down. In a major breach of decorum, Senate Dems boycotted voting sessions on Trump cabinet nominees for Environmental Protection Agency, Treasury, and Health and Human Services. But the worst vitriol was reserved for Education Secretary nominee Betsy DeVos. Here was a perfect target: A woman of considerable wealth, a charter school champion, and a parent who had sent her children to private school could not miss becoming a target of outraged progressives and their teachers' union sponsors.

Coming in a respectable second in the race for most reviled of the Trump cabinet nominees was Senator Jeff Sessions. The veteran senator from Alabama (and most prominent early supporter of Mr. Trump) made history as Senator Cory Booker of New Jersey became the first sitting senator to testify against a colleague's nomination. Senator Booker's hot dog routine was matched by the uber-progressive Senator Elizabeth Warren, who insisted on castigating Mr. Sessions as a racist during floor debate. Ms. Warren would not, in fact, quit her diatribe even after she was warned such character assassination violated Senate debate rules. Her short-term martyrdom was assured after she was rebuked by the full chamber. Said "silencing" was followed by cries of bloody murder from the senator and her supporters. A fundraising letter to the same effect was issued shortly thereafter.

Such antics had little discernible impact on Team Trump. Beginning with the transition, the president-elect remained loyal to his nominees, even when a number of them expressed contrary opinions during Senate confirmation hearings. Media attempts to exploit these differences went nowhere; consistent hostility toward the mainstream media and their storylines was already a well-established Trump attribute. Accordingly, in a reprise of campaign messaging, regular tweets from POTUS continued (all the better to execute a Reaganesque media end around), as did the superlative-laden promises from the polarizing new president.

Unfortunately, unrelenting negative media coverage, especially concerning alleged inappropriate Russian influence during the election, failed to generate more objective analysis of the ways and means of the businessman-president. Few pundits bothered to analyze Trump's full-court press *modus operandi*—a missed opportunity to balance a blitz of one-sided coverage. Leave it to Peggy Noonan's must-read Sunday column in *The Wall Street Journal* (February 9, 2017) to hit the nail squarely on the head: *"Mr. Trump has overloaded all circuits. Everything is too charged, with sparks and small shocks all over."*

A host of to-do items needed to be checked off—the quicker, the better (per the usual velocity of Trump world) while conservative pundits kept close watch over the fate of old campaign promises. But adequate preparation was sometimes lacking for the "get it done" leader. A higher than required price was paid for a poorly vetted executive order on immigration. A galvanized opposition left Republicans confused and embarrassed. Administration officials acknowledged the procedural error, but few Trump supporters were likely lost in the turmoil. Nevertheless, the first substantive miss of the Trump administration was unforced and sloppy. That it led to further organizing by the opposition is without doubt. Now the angry mobs would target Republican "town halls" during the Congressional recess while the media advanced a narrative of "organic" protests breaking out around the country.

But miscalculations and unhelpful narratives don't sidetrack Mr. Trump. Bad press upsets him but does not deter him. His campaign had experienced similar pitfalls—only to survive, even thrive. For Donald Trump, politics is the *ultimate* "art of the deal," only in a different venue than he's used to. For Team Trump, what in its original form appears outrageous may be merely the opening marker in a prolonged negotiation. Opposition overreaction and inaccurate media reports often play into his hands.

No modern politician has adopted a similar approach for fear of sudden (and permanent) political death. But Trump had not previously been a politician. The customs and trappings of the political game are unfamiliar to him. Fans of convention and consistency continue to be forced to take a back seat—*Trump* and *traditional* seldom appear in the same sentence. Even oft-repeated campaign promises can be quickly jettisoned for the greater good (a better "deal").

A timeline of major Trumpian initiatives provides context:

- President-elect Trump browbeat defense contractor Lockheed Martin over the price of the F-35 fighter and suggested he would pit Boeing's comparable F-18 fighter against the F-35 in his decision-making; President Trump's Pentagon spokesman praised a reduced price deal of $8.5 billion for ninety of the state-of-the-art planes.

- Campaigner Trump famously offered a complete ban on Muslim immigration; President Trump imposed a temporary (ninety-day) stay on immigration visas from seven countries with histories of terrorist activities; then, after losing in court, he further narrowed his so-called "extreme vetting" order.

- Campaigner Trump was tough on America's automobile manufacturers, threatening dire consequences for the sin of establishing new facilities in or moving existing ones to Mexico; President Trump offered regulatory relief from Obama-era fuel efficiency standards and major tax breaks while publicly celebrating every time an American manufacturer announced plans to build or expand in the U.S.

- Campaigner Trump targeted union Democrats in the Rust Belt with populist promises of new manufacturing jobs and high tariffs (even a border tax) to fight unfair trade practices; President Trump quickly went about the business of transforming the National Labor Relations Board from a subsidiary of the AFL-CIO to an adjunct of the Chamber of Commerce.

- Campaigner Trump made NAFTA Exhibit A in his campaign against "bad trade deals"; President Trump aimed for "revisions" and "modernization" while requesting increased assistance for border security from the Mexican government.

- Campaigner Trump was hypercritical of U.S. foreign entanglements since 9/11 while advocating an "America First" policy approach on the stump; President Trump gave the Pentagon thirty days to generate a battle plan to engage and defeat ISIS, ordered fifty-nine cruise missiles flown into a Syrian airbase, and used the largest conventional bomb ever assembled to destroy Islamic State tunnels in Afghanistan—all during his first hundred days in office.

- Campaigner Trump repeatedly questioned NATO's relevance and called out many of its members (to their great consternation) for failing to meet their monetary obligations to the alliance; President Trump reaffirmed his support for NATO (including Article 5) and its mission while applauding increased contributions from a number of delinquent member countries.

- Campaigner Trump vowed to label China a "currency manipulator" while citing unfair Chinese trade priorities as a major contributor to America's ever-worsening trade deficit; President Trump jettisoned the "manipulator" tag while conducting a public relations blitz to encourage the Chinese to pacify its missile-testing, saber-rattling client state, North Korea.

- Campaigner Trump strongly opposed "amnesty," especially Mr. Obama's unilaterally imposed "deferred action for childhood arrivals" (DACA) program; President Trump announced he would end DACA, but subject to a six-month extension in order for Congress to address undocumented "Dreamers" in a comprehensive bill.

This was a vastly different narrative from what anyone in Washington, DC, had experienced. "Extreme negotiating" took the political class by storm. The new president could toss many balls in the air at the same time. What was given on one hand could be (quickly) taken away by the other—but usually not in a balanced way. A carrot was often offered to entice. A stick might follow when negotiations bogged down. Yet none of this quelled the press from labeling Trump's first one hundred days as a time of inaction.

A discombobulated establishment attempted to counterattack with a focus on Trump's propensity for repetition, simple language, and over-the-top promises. Such attacks were expected. The anti-politician/businessman had arrived at Campaign 2016 as a veteran *performer* but a rookie *candidate*. He had never run for public office; he had never engaged fellow competitors in public debate; he had rarely ventured into intricate policy discussions outside of his well-known disdain for profligate federal spending, "bad trade deals," and America's seemingly unending foreign entanglements. In campaign debates, he would often engage in rambling, non-germane answers—with plenty of gratuitous insults and asides directed at his opponents. Only a mid-campaign adjustment to more scripted, prepared remarks would prove helpful.

But even Trump detractors—most anyway—were forced to concede that the other side of Trump's public persona was fully capable of serious speechmaking. Admittedly, low expectations played a part—even many Republicans set a low bar in their expectations of Trump's speaking skills. Nevertheless, Trump repeatedly *beat* those expectations while on the world stage (to wit, well-received, powerful speeches to America's Sunni Muslim allies during his initial trip to the Middle East and a Reaganesque appearance before wildly enthusiastic Poles on the heels of a G20 summit in Hamburg, Germany).

More disquieting for media detractors and "Never Trumpers" of all stripes was the timing of such speeches—often delivered while the president was sinking in the polls or experiencing negative press as a result of his latest Twitter war but temporarily "saved" by selected favorable coverage and stronger polling in the aftermath of his high-profile speeches. These "presidential" performances while in the midst of chaos were so Trumplike.

Mass media angst also targeted the president over his foreign policy. Here, a minority of friendly pundits discerned a "strategic ambiguity" (not my phrase) that maintained a resistance to nation-building but also sought strategic advantage through targeted, powerful displays of American military might. But less friendly mainstream observers saw an undisciplined salesman far over his head on the world stage. Whatever one's takeaway, America's friends and enemies alike fully understood this was a very different leader. This president would give autonomy to battlefield commanders while refusing to provide arrival and departure schedules to American enemies. There would be no more leading from behind, but there *would* be more shows of strength and resolve intended for consumption by misbehaving dictators around the world. This was Trump as the anti-Obama in a brand-new foreign policy narrative. He would also happily engage an antagonistic press, often in a personal way, especially when it came to the continuing Trump/Russia campaign storyline. The mainstream media in turn assumed a relentless negativity to just about anything to do with a president it saw as disingenuous, illegitimate, even dangerous. In the process, any remaining pretense of neutrality was lost; much of the mainstream jumped onboard the "resistance" train with little hesitation.

* * *

And so it began. The country buckled in for what promised to be a wild ride—and quickly learned to expect the unexpected.

Throw out the rule book. The political universe is spinning upside down. Nothing is the way it has been.

Let's Make a New Deal

January 24, 2017, *Washington Examiner*

Campaign 2016 will generate years of scholarly analysis, as most expert pundits missed their mark by a wide margin. Few foresaw the advent of a Trump "movement," the long-rumored but never quite completed realignment of the white working class, or the stunning demise of the vaulted Clinton Money Machine. This race was more a WWE grudge match than a political campaign—no surprise to millions of wrestling fans who watched the future president of the United States forcibly shave the head of Vince McMahon at WrestleMania 23.

But "leader of the free world" is not a scripted production. The Oval Office now replaces the rectangular ring. Here, the challenges are quite real. And the bad guys enter not with masks and chairs but with cyber-attacks and ballistic missiles.

On the domestic front, the novice politician/businessman faces a difficult yet opportunity-laden challenge: how to marry traditional Republican philosophy (and constituencies) with the non-traditional views of the Trump coalition—and sustain the marriage in the face of a media and cultural elite fully invested in its failure.

The upside lies in a rare opportunity to jump-start an economy suffering from slow growth and working-class distress—much of it directly related to our overly complex tax code. Both parties recognize that the 73,954 pages of federal tax law acts as a serious drag on economic growth. That it includes a world record–high corporate tax rate of 35 percent makes matters worse. Even Mr. Obama recognized the halting impact of such a high business rate—but refused to do anything about it unless the GOP Congress went along with new social spending. No relief for either side was the unsurprising result.

But minority status tends to sharpen one's focus.

Congressional Democrats could choose to participate by exchanging demands for more social spending with another Democratic priority: infrastructure spending. Interestingly, such a strategy may not be a killer for Republicans who have real infrastructure needs at home. The GOP view would *not* be a function of a Keynesian predicate, however: A low unemployment environment and the recent memory of Obama's failed $1.2 trillion stimulus (with all those not quite "shovel-ready" projects) is not a formula for GOP enthusiasm but, rather, a realization that aging roads, bridges, tunnels, and airports require periodic repairs and upgrades.

Another potential element concerns a bipartisan desire to "bring the dollars home." Approximately $2.1 trillion in corporate profits is presently parked offshore. Numerous high-profile corporate inversions have in turn occurred—to the detriment of the U. S. Treasury. The Obama administration's delusory response was to activate the Treasury's regulatory power to punish rather than work with Congressional Republicans to fix the problem.

A business-savvy Trump administration possesses the wherewithal (and votes) to bring it all together: real reform with fewer brackets and preferences, infrastructure revitalization that meets cost-benefit analysis, a lower corporate tax rate, and a tax holiday whereby repatriated profits would be subject to a reduced rate.

The last comprehensive tax overhaul occurred in 1986 when a conservative president, Ronald Reagan, struck a historic deal with the liberal Speaker Tip O'Neill. Senior players such as Jim Baker, Jack Kemp, and Dan Rostenkowski kept the bill on track—especially when the "losing" economic players to the deal screamed bloody murder. Today's political landscape is more complicated. Partisanship is front and center at all times. And social media makes discreet negotiations far more difficult to conduct. One thing has not changed, however: Strong presidential leadership is essential to getting to "yes." It's all about the art of the deal—so to speak.

The proliferation of safe House seats on both sides of the aisle has given rise to a hyper-partisan Capitol Hill. Today, any enthusiasm to negotiate with the other side is muted by the likelihood of provoking a primary challenge for the offense of "weakness," "softness," or (on the GOP side) "RINO-ness." Accordingly, big-ticket items tend to get accomplished only when the same party controls the House, Senate, and presidency.

With said monopoly power only guaranteed for the next two years, Republican power players would be wise to make their likely once-in-a-generation big-ticket deal as balanced, impactful, and bipartisan as possible.

Recent experience is instructive. A Democratic wave propelled Barack Obama into the presidency and Democrats into control of both Houses of Congress in 2008. Two big-ticket, but poorly produced, bills were shoved through a deeply divided Congress: the aforementioned stimulus (0 GOP House votes, 3 Senate) and the unnatural disaster popularly known as "Obamacare" (0 GOP votes in either House or Senate).

The respective failure of each initiative contributed mightily to the Republican romp of 2010—and to a realignment that has cost Democrats 63 House seats, 10 Senate seats, and 900 state legislative seats over the last six years.

Moral of the story: Big-ticket things can get accomplished under monopoly control, but better things get done (and last longer) when there is buy-in from the other side of the aisle.

Addendum: 2017's tax bill did indeed cut the corporate rate to 21 percent, lower rates for individuals—mostly by doubling the standard deduction—and subject repatriated corporate profits to a one-time rate of 15.5 percent.

From Transformation to Displacement

February 2, 2017, *Washington Examiner*

The unhinged post-election behavior of America's progressives and their media enablers proceeds unabated. Seems the angry reactions of so many cable news pundits during the evening hours of November 8, 2016, have metastasized into daily (if not hourly) attacks on everything Donald J. Trump.

A number of explanations are self-evident. First, the surprising loss of the woman who was pre-ordained to break the proverbial glass ceiling at 1600 Pennsylvania Avenue. Little did the Democratic left anticipate that nearly half of America's female voters would prefer the alleged rogue billionaire with the supermodel (third) wife. Second, *both* party establishments have been shocked by the animus directed to their respective throats by the self-proclaimed leader of a populist "movement." Mr. Trump's inaugural address only added fuel to this antagonistic attitude toward Washington's powers that be. An enthusiasm for confrontation and very public willingness to indulge petty grievances adds to the list of Trump offenses.

Okay, you say, all this is easy to understand. But there must be some other factor—some compelling explanation for the historic inaugural boycotts and unrelenting personal attacks. And you are correct.

Left underanalyzed by the breathless reports of angry millennials and large protest marches is a sense of displacement—not a word you see every day, but nevertheless the appropriate adjective to explain such unrelenting angst.

Webster's defines "displace" as "to move from its usual place." The usual place herein is the recently concluded Obama era, a wonderfully progressive time wherein an unapologetically progressive president did all kinds of progressive things to change our cultural and economic values—to "transform" us into the Western European-style welfare state Mr. Obama and his acolytes envisioned eight years ago.

And so America moved in the desired direction, which was scheduled to be followed by eight additional years of the same from the newly minted progressive Hillary Clinton. Sixteen years of this "usual place" would have indeed changed America forever.

But a bolt of lightning out of nowhere in the form of Donald J. Trump ended the experiment in the blink of an eye. Suddenly, the progressives' New-Age agenda was out—replaced by something very different. To wit:

- The Obama administration's decision to protect "Dreamer" parents through executive order (what the Supreme Court ultimately decided was unconstitutional) was one step, as was the rapid expansion of the illegal immigrant safe havens better known as sanctuary cities. All this was in turn supposed to lead to the ultimate relaxation of our immigration system itself—the so-called "open borders" resolution. Alas, Mr. Trump's proposed wall, strengthened vetting procedures, and opposition to sanctuary jurisdictions have stopped this utopian vision cold.

- Recall Obama's final fastball at Bibi Netanyahu's head in the form of a U.N. step-aside so that the world's Israel haters could have at it one more time over the issue of West Bank housing developments. Of course, progressives applauded the unprecedented move. But even the best-laid plans can go awry. Trump's unabashed pro-Israel views will end talk of a (forced) two- or three-state solution. Further, America will once again step forward as Israel's most reliable ally in a world body full of anti-Semitic Jewish state haters. Note that our Sunni allies are no doubt pleased with this dramatic change of direction. Their quiet accommodation with Israel against ISIS and Shiite Iran will be strengthened under Trump's reign.

- Contrary to what Mr. Obama famously promised the brass at the University of Notre Dame, his administration nevertheless targeted the Catholic hospital-friendly conscience clause (during the Obamacare debate) in order to prove its progressive mettle. In fact, Obama's lawyers went all the way to the Supreme Court to argue that religious freedoms do not follow individuals performing secular activities in the marketplace (the "Hobby Lobby" case)—as though American citizens lose their freedom to follow their religious convictions when performing secular activities (such as filling out insurance policies that include abortion coverage) outside of a religious venue.

The Supreme Court rejected such a proposition, but Hillary Clinton campaigned hard on this "women's issue"—her court would have assuredly flipped the vote here. A Hillary-sponsored court would also have been on a clear path to another campaign promise—abortion on demand. But all of this was not to be. Judge Neil M. Gorsuch, President Trump's nominee to replace the late Antonin Scalia, will sustain a five-vote conservative majority for years to come.

- Teachers' unions viewed the Clinton candidacy as an opportunity to slow the momentum of the school choice movement. After all, hard-line defenders of the indefensible never miss an opportunity to take educational options away from poor parents. But Mr. Trump and his choice of Education Secretary, Betsy DeVos, have far different views. Big-time choice is their mantra. Private vouchers are back on the table. It's now "all of the above" when it comes to failing public schools—which means four (or eight) years of heartburn for the Trump-hating education establishment.

The new president is serious about change, progressive anguish notwithstanding. His inaugural address included the following promise: "We are transferring power from Washington, DC, and giving it back to you, the people." It would be difficult to imagine a more pleasing comment for conservatives; it would be equally difficult to imagine a more disquieting message for the left.

Displacement, indeed.

A Downward Spiral

March 2, 2017, *Washington Examiner*

Character assassination has long been a spectator sport in Washington, DC. Indeed, history buffs regale us with sordid tales of libel, slander, and assorted other methods of reputational damage—committed by the Founding Fathers, no less!

Even our most revered leaders—Lincoln, FDR, Kennedy, and Reagan—engaged or employed surrogates to torch their political opponents and dissenting members of the fourth estate.

I'm in the habit of reminding audiences of such history whenever I hear a questioner bemoan the vitriol associated with today's political discourse. "Nothing much new here" is my typical assurance. But I may soon be forced to change my opinion. It is becoming more difficult to make the case for historical equivalence. Three circumstances unique to the Trump era are to blame.

The first concerns Trump's rhetoric. Our forty-fifth president does not pretend to be a conservative intellectual. He often speaks in simple sentences. Much of what he says is unscripted. He can be vindictive in chastising his opponents—even when wrong on the facts. And apologies for crossing the line are not easily given.

Yet, half of America stands up and applauds every time the president tosses a rhetorical hand grenade at the mainstream media. For these folks, the president's sometimes over-the-top rhetoric is forgiven because they believe he speaks from the heart; that he has the guts to say what they can only think. It's a full-court, anti-PC press—and plenty of flyover deplorables can't seem to get enough of it.

Second, the coarsening of our society proceeds apace. What constitutes socially acceptable language is constantly defined down. The era of censorship seems so 1960s—and it is. Hollywood has played a leading part here, as has social media. And increasing secularization will assuredly deepen our country's cultural permissiveness for the foreseeable future.

A third cause of today's extreme (political) temperature concerns the abrupt exit of President Barack Obama and the equally abrupt arrival of the anti-Obama Trump. Many on the left assumed a Clinton win would continue the Obama era's leftward lurch. Talk about a dream agenda. Clinton promised a progressive Supreme Court, abortion on demand, open borders, sanctuary cities, transgender bathrooms—even an end to that outdated notion of "American exceptionalism."

But an extended progressive era came crashing down on November 8. And it was the uncouth, bombastic nationalist who did it. No wonder the rhetoric has been so overboard. Everybody hates the party pooper!

There is an especially grotesque element of contemporary (political) communication that further soils our discourse: the gratuitous use of "Nazi" or "racist" whenever conservatives advocate a position adverse to the progressives' adopted moral high ground.

Full disclosure here includes a President-elect Trump who took the bait when he compared intelligence leaks regarding a Russian-produced dossier on his private life to Nazi Germany. The reviews were less than positive; throw the flag on the president for that one. But progressives are the overwhelming winners of the Nazi/racist race to the bottom. Google searches of "Nazi" and "racist" and "fill-in-the-blank Republican" will keep one busy for many hours.

And so month two of the Trump era begins with these and similar indictments lodged against the president by America's leading academics, actors, artists, and pundits. Their nullification campaign continues. The escalating nature of the rhetoric is evident. The media's shockingly positive response to Trump's first speech to a joint session of Congress notwithstanding, de-escalation does not appear to be an option. How is a reasonable person to interpret all the daily noise?

The answer is clear—but easier said than done. We consumers of news must become more critical in our daily interpretation of what we see and read.

A few examples from the past few weeks provide helpful context:

- The president insults CNN or one of its reporters. That's an easy one—an (almost) daily occurrence.
- The president plans to deploy 100,000 National Guard troops in nationwide immigration raids. This storyline is plausible, but better to investigate further. Oops, turns out the AP published a false story on the basis of a draft memo; the news agency subsequently apologized.
- The president removes a bust of Dr. Martin Luther King from the Oval Office on the eve of his inauguration. This just didn't sound right from the jump. And it was not true—just a bit of fake news—all the better to fit a racist narrative.

Gen-Xers and millennials are expert at trolling social media outlets. They can figure it out for themselves. For my fellow baby boomers—the bad news is that Walter Cronkite is not coming back. The good news is that most of us can still recognize a stinker when we see one—but we just have to dig a bit deeper.

Have you students of history heard of the Thousand Days' War? Well, welcome to the "Four Years' War"! And slurs and melodrama have replaced truth as the first casualty.

The Trump Era's 5 Emerging Constituencies

March 30, 2017, *Washington Examiner*

My travels around the country provide continuing exposure to how the country is responding to our new president. Included in this learning is information about how average Americans are coping with the dramatic new production "The Donald Comes to Washington."

On second thought, "dramatic" may be too understated an adjective. Rarely has America witnessed such a radical turnabout in such a brief period of time. Yet even at this early stage, one can discern how various factions are coming together, or falling apart, in response to the Trump era. These five emerging constituencies are numerous and subtle and require further analysis.

First in line are the "haters"—foot soldiers of the "resistance—ready and willing to show up at a moment's notice at any flavor of Trump protest. They are the "mad as hell and not going to take it anymore" crowd. Some (most) continue in a state of electoral semi-denial. They understand Trump won but just can't bring themselves to accept all of the new realities (real or imagined) they must confront. A fair percentage of this group live in liberal enclaves along the coasts. Many of them do not know anyone who voted for Trump. Note that more than a few had no love lost for Hillary Clinton. These true believers were bothered by the Clintonian propensity to bend and parse the truth. Most would have preferred Bernie Sanders or Elizabeth Warren.

This hardcore opposition manifests an abiding animosity toward the new president. They have a deep dislike of "Trump the person" surpassed only by their disdain for "Trump the politician." A few even long for the days of "W"—and they *really* hated him. The piece-by-piece dismantling of Obama's progressive machinery will make the next four years difficult indeed.

The next group in the queue is rather small by comparison. There is no apparent leader and they do not draw the type of media attention reserved for the haters. These are the disappointed (but not trans-fixed) Clinton liberals hoping for an accommodation with Trump on issues of common concern (trade, child care, border tax, infra-structure improvements, no entitlement reform). Most are bothered by the illiberal shouting down of alternative voices on campus. They know that real liberals do not countenance such anti-speech behav-ior. Members of this group came of age during the great protest movements of the 1960s; such antics remain antithetical to their core beliefs.

Next in line are the "Never Trumpers." Yes, they are still around, if diminished. Included herein are some elements of what used to be known as the "Republican establishment"—before it was run over by Trump's "movement." Similar to group one, members herein are still dazed by Trump's *modus operandi* and victory. Its members continue to profess embarrassment over the president's ad hoc actions and willingness to engage petty beefs. But they also see a framework of conservative policies much to their liking. Not so long ago, members of this group could never envision a pro-life, pro-gun, tax-cutting regulatory reformer in the person of a billionaire real estate mogul who willingly and notoriously contributed big dollars to liberal Democrats and made no effort to hide or apologize for such behavior while running for president on the GOP ticket.

Constituency number four is larger and less angst-ridden. These are the generally conservative Republicans who had supported one of the seventeen other candidates during the Republican primaries before "coming home" as the general election approached. Some arrived in the Trump camp ready to work; others steered clear of the celebrity candidate until the potential reality of another Clin-ton presidency kick-started them onto the Trump bandwagon. These folks are generally happy with the Trump cabinet and early policy initiatives but are driven to distraction by the constant tweets that (sometimes) take the president far off message. The most cited advice I receive from this crowd: "Can't you just get him to stop taking the bait—or better yet stop the tweets?!" My questioners are displeased but not surprised by my negative response.

Finally, we come to what will be the most overanalyzed sub-grouping of the lot—the "true believers." They are the working-class folks who early on fell in love with Trump's heated populism—and unabashed nationalism. Many are frustrated Democrats who have long found themselves out of sync with their party's leftward drift. Some are conservatives moved by the thought of a pro-business president. You know, somebody who has signed the front of a payroll check. Others are libertarians pleased by the administration's lack of interest in most social issues. The latter two groupings constitute approximately 40 to 45 percent of the country. They live in (mostly) red states. They put up with Trump's often uncouth manner; they love his lack of political correctness. It is they who will have a major say in whether Donald J. Trump is "fired" or given another four-year contract.

Time for the GOP to Get Moving

April 20, 2017, *Washington Examiner*

My previous column, "The Trump Era's 5 Emerging Constituencies," critiqued the emerging political constituencies of the Trump era. Today's chronicles the major challenges confronting our two major parties as a divided nation seeks to find its way forward.

For the Democrats, circa 2016 conventional wisdom viewed Hillary Clinton as a slam-dunk winner. Her campaign was to be a reaffirmation of Obama-style progressivism—and the importance of changing demographics. Most pundits foresaw a celebratory coming of age for Obama's coalition: younger, hip, secular, and *very* liberal. A large turnout of minority voters (especially Hispanics) would ensure the demise of Donald J. Trump. The flip side was thought to be etched in stone—a death by demographics for the old, white, conservative, fossil fuel-powered GOP. That dinosaur had enjoyed a long run. But it was now time to step aside for a new generation sure to dominate presidential cycle voting for the foreseeable future.

On policy, the demonstrated shortcomings of Obama's signature legislative achievements (Obamacare, Dodd-Frank, Stimulus) would not deter Democrats from doubling down on anti-market initiatives. Indeed, DNC Chair Debbie Wasserman Schultz was hard pressed to cite a difference between her Democrats and socialism during a now infamous appearance on MSNBC's *Hardball* in July of 2015. But use of the adjective "infamous" requires further definition: Ms. Wasserman-Schultz's answer was panned *only* on the right. Few within the Democratic coalition bothered to contest their leader's refusal to answer the question. And all of this prior to uber-progressive Senators Bernie Sanders and Elizabeth Warren assuming rock star status on the campaign trail.

It all sounded so good on paper—and even better when it became apparent Ms. Clinton would run to the left of Obama. In striking contrast to her triangulating husband, she made it clear the "era of big government" was here to stay. No more searching for a middle ground on abortion. No more questioning of sanctuary cities or the open borders crowd. And forget all those private speeches to the captains of investment and industry (at $250,000 per); Wall Street was about to become "Enemy #1" for the American worker.

But left out of the equation (purposefully, it appears) was that shrinking-yet-essential white working-class constituency held over from the Roosevelt era. These are the predominately ethnic, Catholic, and socially conservative foot soldiers of a New Deal coalition that lasted for approximately half a century—until Ronald Reagan. Thirty-five years later, their remaining affinity for Democrats came to an official end. Too many had suffered at the hands of a no-growth economy. They *still* believed in the American Dream. They cling to the notion of American exceptionalism. They want a "wall" and a declaration of war against radical Islam. That so many of them lived in the Rust Belt and were so unhappy with the status quo was relegated to secondary status. Such became the fatal flaw in the Clinton calculus.

It seems unlikely the Democrats are willing or likely to change direction. One day (post-election) I was waiting for an interview on MSNBC while listening to a Democratic member of Congress as he vowed to learn a lesson (from the election) and henceforth listen to the people. Shortly thereafter, that same Democrat repeated his unqualified support for sanctuary cities...so goes the progressive take on working-class values.

The Trump presidency presents Republicans with equally challenging obstacles. The president's direct and sometimes inartful messaging continues to antagonize some GOPers—especially those who have been less than enthusiastic about Trump from the jump. Mr. Trump's propensity to take names and shots at those who oppose him (including members of Congress he will need in the future) is not an effective long-term strategy.

Moreover, and notwithstanding the above-cited Democratic challenges, rapidly changing demographics and continued cultural permissiveness constitute very real threats to America's center-right party. Approximately two-thirds of a rapidly growing Hispanic constituency is now reliably Democratic. And the engrained social liberalism of the Obama years is unlikely to change in light of Mr. Trump's lack of interest in most social issues.

Far more daunting for GOP prospects is the *vibe* of the Trump movement. His rallies were/are more akin to revival meetings. But high-octane rhetoric produces high expectations. The customers now expect a return on their emotional (and voting) investment. And a fever pitch is difficult to maintain over four years. What to do?

Well, one sure way to beat an unfriendly demographic tide is to do something productive. Newly sworn-in Justice Neil Gorsuch was a nice first step. A willingness to use U.S. military might against the world's miscreants is also a welcome change from Obama-era disengagement and the slow start to tax reform. But reducing health care premiums and growing the economy are the real "have-tos" this term.

Few will stress over the not-ready-for-primetime Obamacare "replace" effort once legislation actually moves. Remember: Really big things tend to get done in hyper-partisan Washington when one party possesses the cards.

Time for the GOP to move.

It's the Little Things

April 29, 2017, *Washington Examiner*

Lost among all the scorecards surrounding President Trump's "First 100 Days" and the big-stakes issues of Obamacare repeal and tax reform is an appreciation for the "smaller things that count." These are the under-the-radar events that do not generate daily headlines but reflect a new and very different path for America going forward.

- You may have missed Trump's decision to "fire" the American Bar Association as the official vetter of judicial nominees. Most Americans (including many attorneys) are unaware of the hard left-leaning predisposition(s) of this powerful governing body. But conservatives know it well—and are now presented with a rare opportunity to do something about it.
- There are currently 20 U.S. Appeals Court and 99 District Court vacancies throughout the country. A Republican majority controls the United States Senate. Hence, conservatives have been presented with a historic opportunity to reshape the judicial landscape for decades to come. It now falls to Senate Majority Leader Mitch McConnell to make it happen. The sooner the better for those of us concerned about the unapologetic judicial activism advanced by so many Obama appointees.
- Recall the Obama administration's last cheap shot at Israel wherein the U.S. failed to veto a United Nations resolution condemning Bibi Netanyahu's settlement building on the West Bank. Accompanying the embarrassing veto was Secretary of State John Kerry's own parting shot wherein Israel was taken to task for its failure to support a two-state resolution.

Far more under the radar was Obama's midnight authorization of $221 million to the Palestinian Authority (PA). All three acts reflected the Obama administration's well-known disregard for Netanyahu's right-wing government.

Alas, the arrival of the unabashedly pro-Israel Trump administration has brought a welcome change in U.S. policy—and a freeze on the PA's Obama cash. How refreshing. The PA's propensity to make nice with terrorists operating in the Gaza Strip (including paying the families of jihadists who die as martyrs) is well established. Such behavior should never be subsidized by the American taxpayer. Closer to home, we can hope that America's Johnny-come-lately support for Netanyahu and his government will slow the momentum of campus leftists in their campaign(s) to force divestment of Israeli companies from university portfolios. Such economic boycotts are the latest example of progressive enmity focused on the Jewish state.

- Political junkies of a certain age will recall Newt Gingrich's "Contract with America" circa 1994. A number of its provisions sought to unchain private enterprise from the confines of the regulatory state. One such exercise was a "corrections day" process whereby obsolete or hurtful regulations were identified for elimination by unanimous bipartisan vote—a worthy goal but a bridge too far for many House liberals. Accordingly, few such regulations bit the dust. Nevertheless, a foundation for regulatory relief had been established. One year later, the Congressional Review Act was passed. Henceforth, Congress was given the power to reject final agency rules within sixty days of their publication.

The act remained mostly dormant for twenty years (President George W. Bush used it once) until Donald J. Trump came to town. The new administration has worked with the GOP Congress to roll back thirteen (primarily eleventh-hour) Obama regulations—covering everything from coal mining to gun rights. Note that the CRA is more powerful than people realize: The offending agency is forbidden from issuing similar rules once the rule at issue has been killed.

Elimination of overreaching or counterproductive rules is an essential but underappreciated plank in Trump's effort to unleash economic growth. Success here does not tend to produce headlines as the mainstream media insists on measuring an executive's success by the number of new laws enacted—and how much government grew over a certain period of time. But most members of *this* Congressional majority measure effectiveness by how much government shrank. They ran on this platform and mean to see their promises fulfilled. This disconnect between a Republican administration and a left-leaning media is one to keep in mind as Trump's "grades" are handed out.

- Lost among the heated rhetoric surrounding the president's long-promised southern wall/fence is a significant drop in illegal border crossings. The number of unaccompanied minors has similarly decreased in dramatic fashion. And all of this without a long-overdue immigration bill or the hiring of additional border agents.

A logical takeaway is that even those who deal in human trafficking read the papers. They see a new sheriff in Washington—one (finally) serious about our porous southern border. Ten years of contentious debate about sovereignty and open borders has made many Americans question the government's commitment to immigration enforcement. Here's hoping the president's powerful use of his bully pulpit will restore trust in the rule of law.

These are simply a sampling of reports reflecting America's new and very different path. There are many such small steps taking place on a daily basis. As they say, elections have consequences. Indeed, they do.

Like Him or Not, Trump Is Now a Member
of the Republican Family

July 11, 2017, *Washington Examiner*

The aftermath of the special election in Georgia's 6th Congressional district has been predictably brutal. Critical reviews from the progressive hinterlands have littered social media after yet another Trump-era special election defeat for the Democrats.

The ferocity of the criticism speaks to partisan frustration; this district was supposed to be chock-full of suburban Republicans just itching for an opportunity to register their disdain for Trump. But the depth of "Trump trauma" was far less than advertised; a late Trump endorsement may have even helped newly elected Rep. Karen Handel, R-Ga.

For the Democrats, two problematic narratives have emerged:

1. What if the Russian hacking/Trump story continues to go south?
2. What if a more moderate message is not a winning message in suburban swing districts?

You can bet each scenario has the attention of Democratic operatives desperately searching for a winning strategy against a supposedly vulnerable Trump.

A related and equally interesting high-stakes discussion is playing out on the other side of the aisle. And it has been on my mind since a significant percentage of the "loyal opposition" shifted into resistance mode during the late evening hours of November 8, 2016.

The conversation pertains to a condition (henceforth to be called "family syndrome") that afflicts a subset of Republicans who have never been enthusiastic participants in Team Trump. These are predominately conservatives who supported other GOP candidates in the primaries and were latecomers to the Trump bandwagon.

Post-election, they are generally pleased with Trump policy (especially the promotion of Neil Gorsuch to the Supreme Court), but remain ambivalent (or worse) with just about everything else connected to this president and his unorthodox methods of operation. Most have grown weary of the daily drama that defines the Trump White House.

Yet, the vast majority have stuck with Trump, and it is not merely because of common ground on most issues. They are digging in for the same reason that family can criticize family—but not so much outsiders. Most of you are familiar with the phenomenon.

Truth be told, these Republicans willingly and regularly engage in Trump bashing amongst themselves. They are often reminded (sometimes by Trump himself) that he is no lifelong Republican or movement conservative. And they remain uncomfortable with the edginess, the petty beefs, the daily tweets, and the relentless media bashing.

Nevertheless, the president remains (albeit new) family and the party leader, after eight agonizing years in the desert. And so Trump trashing generally remains an intramural sport. When outsiders seek to indulge, an instinctive defensiveness is triggered: Wagons are circled; foxholes are dug. It's a doubling down in support of this most unlikely Republican president—yet another fascinating aspect of Trump's unique appeal.

In the real world, this defensiveness plays out in many ways. Often, the offended right-winger seeks to magnify opposition misdeeds. In the case of progressive Democrats (and Hillary Clinton particularly), generally, there is no shortage of such travails. This exercise also tends to minimize Trump's flaws. After all, he's our guy, he's under relentless attack, and now is not the time to talk outside the family (so to speak). Here, marginal supporters ratchet up their emotional capital invested in Trump. This reservoir of support in turn will make it harder to divest when times turn difficult.

In this context, embarrassing episodes such as the recent CNN-sponsored fake news story on alleged links between a Trump confidant and a Russian bank only serve to deepen the reservoir. This will typically be the result when the "Hate Trump Always" members of the media are shown to be wrong, negligent, and sloppy in reporting on Trump.

It's fair to ask how long this protectiveness can last. Persistent, ugly conflict with the mainstream media and our cultural elites could at some point simply exhaust this constituency—or lessen the desire to circle the wagons yet again. Still, with no moderate Democrat on the horizon, it will take a lot of turmoil for GOP partisans to willingly take a pass on Trump.

My fellow Republicans should feel free to test my theory. The next time one of your conservative friends starts to complain about Trump's latest outburst or tweet, tell him that you agree—and that you watched the very same criticism of Trump from Bernie Sanders, Elizabeth Warren, Hillary Clinton, Nancy Pelosi, Chuck Schumer, Debbie Wasserman Schultz, or Keith Ellison on CNN the previous evening. Then, stand aside and watch the sudden change of heart. ("What? They can't talk about the president like that!") This might be followed by an aggressive, possibly even passionate, defense of the same man they were tearing apart just a minute ago.

All of which may give Trump a longer-lasting reign than his multitude of critics could possibly imagine.

Legislators with Black Robes

August 8, 2017, *Washington Examiner*

Our politics is consumed by the daily circus surrounding the Trump administration. The president's unorthodox style drives the train and churns the Washington press corps (and the country) daily, hourly.

It's all quite good for television ratings, but not so helpful for substance. Indeed, few voters bother with the complexities of legislative agendas or policy minutiae when new press secretaries are coming and going weekly. In the process, the next incarnation of Obamacare or the initial outline of a comprehensive tax overhaul receives second billing compared to what the president tweeted that morning—especially if the tweet contradicts what another administration spokesperson said the previous day.

Still, moving policy forward remains the most important measure of any administration. Here, legislative victories count, as do regulatory reforms that undo Obama-era overreach.

But less attention is given to judicial wins—the all-important opinions issued by lifetime appointees in charge of our co-equal branch of government.

For immediate context, think about how a few thousand voters in Wisconsin, Pennsylvania, and Michigan made it possible for Neil Gorsuch (rather than Merrick Garland) to become the all-important "fifth vote" on an evenly divided Supreme Court. Now that I have your attention, give some thought to your views on the following questions:

- Whether a subdivision (or state) that refuses to cooperate with federal immigration officials in the identification and detention of those living here illegally should lose federal funding?

- Whether local boards of election can require everyone who shows up at a poll to produce some form of photo identification in order to cast a ballot?

- Whether a commercial baker should be required to cater a same-sex wedding (or a photographer required to take pictures at it) if the owner of the commercial establishment opposes same-sex marriage on religious grounds?
- Whether contractors should be required to disclose allegations that it violated federal labor law when bidding on new federal contracts?
- Whether a pastor should be required to comply with a subpoena demanding copies of sermons (pertaining to controversial social issues) delivered to a congregation?
- Whether an Asian-American rock band that deliberately took its name from an insulting racial slur ("The Slants") should be provided trademark protection from the U.S. Patent and Trademark Office?

These queries are a mere sampling of the divisive questions presented to our courts; each gut-wrenching issue is the focal point of a past or present lawsuit. A few have already gone all the way to the Supreme Court.

How courts decide these matters will be determined by an intelligent (at least on paper) group of individuals who have enjoyed similar legal training but who maintain deeply held differences when it comes to their job description. Here, the endless complexities of the law are broken down to a single question: Are you an "originalist" or "activist"? Alternatively, do you confine your legal opinions to the plain text of the law or do you take the law in the direction you believe it should go?

Those who subscribe to the former philosophy are buoyed by the willingness of the president and Congressional Republicans to reverse unilaterally imposed Obama-era policy. Here, eight years of significant damage to our economy is in the process of being cleaned up by aggressive GOP-led regulatory teams (not bashful about utilizing the

Congressional Review Act) that have achieved dramatic success in Mr. Trump's first seven months. Some pundits believe Congressional willingness to take down so much Obama administration regulatory overreaching is a major reason for the run-up in the stock market since Election Day 2016. I don't doubt it.

But using the rules to kill off burdensome regulations has its limits. And those limitations can be found in the 329 federal judges (including two Supreme Court justices) appointed during the Obama years. These appointments mean Obama's appointees will be engaging their inner activist selves for many years to come.

This should be a timely reminder to the "Never Trump" crowd. There are thousands of ambitious, uber-progressive young attorneys out there just waiting in the wings for the next Democratic president/Senate—just waiting for their opportunity to unleash another barrage of progressive ideas on our culture and country—if we let them.

It will not be easy for anyone to keep their eye on the ball through all the Trump-generated drama. The Democrats smell blood in the water. The aforementioned GOP detractors remain none too pleased. But it must be done. Confining the next generation of progressive activists to the minor leagues and out of our courtrooms is an imperative. Republicans and conservatives forget this notion at their own peril—the country forgets this notion at a major cost to an America (already) at risk.

Trump Making Tons of Progress While the Media Ignores It

September 15, 2017, *Washington Examiner*

The Trump presidency has been eventful so far, to say the least. The new president's *modus operandi* is truly unique—guaranteed to ruffle the Washington establishment's feathers for as long as he is around. Accordingly, every day is chock-full of Twitter blasts, personnel changes, resistance-inspired demonstrations, and, of course, everything and anything to do with investigations into Russian President Vladimir Putin's election-hacking ways.

But "frustrating" may best define the new president. To wit, the same man who garnered Reaganesque comparisons during high-profile foreign trips to the Middle East and Europe can also be his own worst enemy.

The Charlottesville episode is instructive. Words of condemnation after neo-Nazis and related groups cause a riot are not difficult; just condemn neo-Nazi nutjobs with specificity in the strongest terms. The responsibility of wing-nut leftists such as "Antifa" can be appropriately condemned at a later time and place. What was widely interpreted as a less than overwhelming initial response led to weeks of bad press. Such is the product of an unforced error.

An unproductive Congress contributes to the uneasiness. The left clings to the notion that the arc of history remains with them (the short-term annoyance of Trump notwithstanding), so strident opposition defines their every move. On the other side, a disjointed GOP struggles to move major bills—and is conflicted as to how to work with a president who will cut deals with Democrats just as easily as with Republicans.

But this column is not about baneful Democrats, bashful Republicans, media dust-ups, the latest Hollywood lefty threatening to leave the country, or even the president's disinclination for politics-as-usual.

Rather, I offer an inventory of underanalyzed, unilateral U-turns undertaken during the initial stages of the Trump administration.

Illegal Immigration

Too much back-and-forth analysis regarding the long-promised "wall" has diverted attention from the fundamental issue: how best to restore security to our southern border. Yet illegal border crossings are down dramatically. It appears that jawboning from the president and improved morale among border patrol officers has made a difference. Who would have thought human traffickers watch *Hannity*?

Legal Immigration

The often-vilified H1B visa program for skilled foreign workers was set up in order to fill positions left unfilled by American workers. The program has grown over the years (driven by support from U.S. technology companies) but now faces renewed scrutiny from a Trump administration serious about enforcement of our immigration laws. Recent media reports reflect an uptick in government requests for supporting documentation, especially for entry-level wage applicants. All of which comports with the administration's focus on how illegal, low-skilled workers undermine U.S. labor markets.

Ballot Security

Republican-supported ballot security initiatives have sprung up around the country to much progressive angst. The most popular measure is "voter photo ID"—a ballot security measure that had been a favorite target of progressives (especially Obama's Department of Justice). Still, Democratic resistance to what should be no-brainer measures is ongoing. Seems that few on the left care to recognize how easy it is to obtain photo identification in today's world (just go to any DMV) or how many of our modern institutions require photo identification be supplied upon request. Fortunately, it appears that progressives' "racist" indictment against verifiable photo identification measures is losing steam. It's about time.

Housing

The Obama-era Department of Housing and Urban Development was deeply interested in preempting local zoning ordinances. The narrative is familiar: Pick any subdivision where racial housing patterns are not to the federal government's liking, accuse the locals of discriminatory zoning practices, then negotiate a "settlement" that mandates the construction of new low-cost housing units even where there is no evidence of discrimination and the challenged local zoning laws are shown to be race-neutral. This mindset is a major departure from the notion that people should be free to live where they can afford to live. It is expected that Ben Carson's HUD will reestablish this view. Score one for common sense, restored.

Environment

In no particular order, the Trump administration has begun dismantling Obama's Clean Power Plan, reversed controversial federal monument land set-asides, withdrawn from the Paris Climate Accord, expedited pipeline construction, and championed American exports of liquefied natural gas. Trump is the anti-Obama in many respects, none more so than when it comes to energy exploration and independence.

Labor Relations

The Obama-era National Labor Relations Board had employers in its crosshairs for eight long years. That body sought to extend joint employer status to independent contractors (and franchisors), expand mandatory dues schemes, mandate disclosure demands on business owners, coerce workers into supporting union-organized elections, and double the weekly threshold for salaried workers to be exempt from overtime (a rule recently overturned by a federal judge and one that Obama's Labor Department admitted would require 2.5 million hours of additional paperwork alone). Today, Obama's job-killing machine is in the process of being shut down by a new Trump-designated Republican majority—yet another reason employers are feeling more confident about the future these days.

Net Neutrality

Trump's new Federal Communications Commission chairman, Ajit Pai, is looking to overturn the Obama FCC's finding that the internet is more telecommunications service than information service. Few issues distinguish economic free marketers from centralized regulators more than this one. And a large segment of the public is paying close attention: The FCC received 21 million comments on Pai's proposal to reverse the Obama FCC's heavy-handed approach to telecom service. There is now solid evidence that reclassification has negatively impacted broadband build-out. Maybe, just maybe, freedom will win another round here too.

Addendum: Chairman Pai got his wish on a 3–2 vote on December 14, 2017.

Israel

The Jewish state again has a reliable friend in the Oval Office. The timing is perfect, as a historic coalition of the U.S., Israel, and leading Sunni Muslim allies band together to oppose a terror-enabling Iranian regime and its chief sponsor, Russia. Out of sight and out of mind is the Obama administration's strong animus toward Israeli Prime Minister Benjamin Netanyahu and his Likud Party. No wonder the Israeli prime minister seemed almost giddy during his initial sit-down with Trump. A bit of icing on the cake: Trump's rescission of Obama's last-second $221 million gift to the PLO.

Title IX

Obama's Department of Education used the law to significantly narrow due process rights for those accused of sexual harassment or sexual assault on campus. The changes included "guidance" requiring the lowering of a complainant's burden of proof from "clear and convincing" to a "preponderance of the evidence" standard. Of greater concern to some is the practice of discouraging accused students from cross-examination of their accuser (in order to prevent the trauma of confrontation). The reliably left-leaning American Bar Association has raised concerns regarding the new, lower burden of proof, while many observers have serious concerns with a process that seeks to limit cross-examination rights in these often emotional cases. Note also that dozens of wrongfully accused students have successfully brought suit against their colleges over the past few years. New Education Secretary Betsy DeVos has promised to level the playing field—to the shock and dismay of progressive activists.

Cuba

Fewer American resources are going to prop up Raúl Castro's despotic regime. The president's reversal of the Obama administration's liberalized business and tourism guidelines may have upset American businesses seeking new markets, but, in classic Trump verbiage, "This was a bad deal." In fact, in classic Obama terms, it was a one-way deal—no repatriation of wanted criminals, no relief for imprisoned human rights dissidents or persecuted prisoners of faith, no progress toward compensation for (long) aggrieved private property owners. Political note: Those who perpetrated the notion that Obama's outreach would be a political winner for Hillary Clinton among Floridians of Cuban descent should check voter totals from Little Havana on Election Day.

Trump Is Already Beating Obama in the Most Important Ways

September 25, 2017, *Washington Examiner*

The editorial pages are beginning to devote more column space to the election of 2020. It's all about President Trump, of course—specifically, how Democrats smell blood in the water, and how they intend to sell their reconfigured platform to voters. The narrative includes an assurance that next time they will not nominate a pretend Johnny (or Jane)-come-lately progressive such as Hillary Clinton, but the real thing—aka Bernie Sanders or Elizabeth Warren.

Observers can think about the political calculus this way: Trump is the denominator, a baseline for everything and anything that progressives believe went awry commencing on January 20. The numerators will be a familiar list of progressive causes: single-payer health care (already a priority item for potential Democratic presidential candidates), abortion on demand, a $15 minimum wage, loose border and voter identification requirements, sanctuary cities, a war on fossil fuels, and funding cuts to charter schools.

Just how Democrats will go about selling their "Progressive 2.0" program to the socially and economically conservative working class remains to be seen, especially if "Trumpanomics" manages to produce anything close to sustained growth. What is likely not to occur due to all the Trump-related drama is a serious re-examination of Obama-era miscalculations and strategic errors. But keeping track of what just happened, and why, is important for a sharply divided country.

The Economy

Let's begin with good old-fashioned economic growth—oxygen for politicians looking to create good times and happy constituents. That both were in short supply as President Barack Obama arrived in the White House is without doubt. The historic recession that followed the mortgage meltdown set America on its heels, and was a significant factor in Obama's convincing win over Senator John McCain in 2008.

But Obama's highly ballyhooed Keynesian prescriptions did not work. It is now a matter of economic history that his preemptive regulatory assault, tax increases, and monstrous $1.2 trillion stimulus failed to kick-start the post-recession economy. In fact, the Obama administration's primary economic "accomplishments" were to diminish labor participation (degraded to 1970s levels) and double the federal budget deficit. Some pundits believe Obama's slow growth record contributed mightily to Hillary Clinton's defeat in usually Democratic Rust Belt states. I agree. The working class never got around to accepting Obama's 1.5 percent growth as the new normal, despite a persistent media narrative that they do so.

Conversely, gross domestic product growth under Trump is approaching 3 percent. Note this is prior to passage of a tax bill that has economic commentators predicting the Dow Jones Industrial Average to reach 25,000. At least initially, the business community has responded enthusiastically to Trump's deregulatory, market-orientated approach.

Health Care

The manmade disaster better known as Obamacare represents another low point in Obama's forecaster curve. The now infamous promise that you could keep your doctor and your health care and that the average family would end up saving $2,500 per year was repeated ad nauseam—and was subsequently awarded *PolitiFact's* "Lie of the Year." Notwithstanding the GOP's inept attempts to repeal and replace, a movie still playing at a theater near you, it was a well-earned (dis)honor.

Immigration

On immigration, you may recall Obama poking fun at border enforcement, joking that perhaps the border patrol should construct a "moat" to deter illegal crossings. (The cost of illegal immigration to the taxpayer was not deemed a funny enough topic, and so was not mentioned.) That same president repeatedly assured us that try as he might, he lacked the authority to unilaterally grant amnesty to Dreamers or any similarly situated group. When this reminder of constitutional limitation failed to placate his base, he simply flip-flopped and did it anyway—at least until the courts stopped him.

Trump set a far different course. He seeks to defund sanctuary cities, refocus immigration policy on skilled immigrants, and declines to enforce the aforementioned unconstitutional order on Dreamers (preferring instead that Congress actually do its job and pass a bill). Early results are promising. There has been a dramatic decrease in illegal border crossings under Trump, an accomplishment achieved prior to construction of his long-promised "beautiful wall." Seems the border patrol has responded to a leader that has its back, and the numbers reflect it.

Foreign Policy

Obama's foreign policy record is similarly replete with naïve prescriptions and policy missteps. A first-year "apology tour" made Obama popular in foreign venues but failed to charm miscreant dictators into changing their behavior. An early "reset" with Russia proved unproductive, as did a well-publicized outreach to gulag-friendly Raúl Castro. A nuclear deal with Iran was struck, but the mullahs in Tehran continue to be the primary funders of terror in the world while a "Shiite crescent" casts a foreboding shadow over the Middle East.

A diplomatic pivot to China was heavily hyped but unsuccessful; the Chinese Navy doubled down on its provocations in the South China Sea. In Egypt, a bet on the Muslim Brotherhood quickly turned sour; an extended Arab Spring was diminished in the process. In Iraq, a military surge produced a victory soon compromised by an insistence on (premature) American withdrawal. Meanwhile, a weapons of mass destruction-inspired "red line" intended to intimi-date the murderous Bashar Assad regime in Syria became a punchline for American inaction in the face of evil. Speaking of Assad's reign of terror, Obama's musings about how Russian involvement in Syria would prove to be its own Vietnam missed the mark by a wide mar-gin. By the summer of 2017, Russian military might had turned the tide of war on behalf of the embattled dictator.

The anti-war inclinations of the anti-war Obama never changed. His vision was undergirded by a reflexive willingness to placate bad guys (and therefore avoid conflict), including a propensity to provide the precise timetable for American withdrawal from the battlefield. Yet, what was intended to prevent future quagmires ended up being appreciated far more by our enemies than our friends.

These prominent remembrances from Obama's tenure are instructive as the Democrats and their media allies begin to trans-form the "resistance" into a progressive campaign vehicle for 2020. But the rest of us should recall a familiar axiom: "Those who do not learn history are doomed to repeat it." Going forward, the country must not forget its recent past.

Chaotic White House Aside, Trump Is Achieving Reaganesque Policy Wins

October 20, 2017, *Washington Examiner*

A fascinating intraparty fracture is developing within the Republican Party. Of course, it concerns President Trump, but what doesn't in Washington, DC, these days?

This one is not so much about the GOP establishment versus Trump—although that storyline is legitimate. Suffice to say there are many Republicans in Washington (and elsewhere) who have seriously ruffled feathers concerning the president's independent ways and accompanying general disregard for their feelings. The rift is not difficult to understand. To repeat: Trump is and remains more movement leader than partisan chieftain; he has shown an unsurprising willingness to throw Republican members of Congress under the bus when it suits his greater purpose. Those who expect an attitudinal adjustment by the commander-in-chief will most likely be disappointed.

A far more important divide is deserving of your attention, however. It concerns the growing dichotomy between what many observers see as a chaotic White House on the one hand, and a Reaganesque flair for gritty policy calls on the other. Peggy Noonan's most recent Sunday column was devoted to the former as she described how (many) Republican Senators remain at a loss to deal with a free agent president resistant to control—even by senior staff.

The narrative includes criticisms that have grown familiar during Trump's first year in office. Here, the president is viewed as a shoot-from-the-hip neophyte too undisciplined to govern and quite dangerous in a world populated by despots who wield nuclear weapons.

Senator Bob Corker's recent broadsides qualify here. The retiring Republican Senator from Tennessee sees an overmatched executive lacking in "competence" and "stability," albeit surrounded by a competent senior group daily engaged in the task of keeping the leader of the free world from careening off the rails. (Whatever did happen to keeping family disputes within the family?)

Make no mistake, this is how today's Washington views the president and his administration. Note that this particular indictment is distinguished from the "all hands on deck" Trump haters who continue to be transfixed by a Trump/Russian collusion conspiracy story that lacks credible supporting evidence after two years of exhaustive investigation and desperate mainstream media attention.

In striking contrast are a series of Trump administration policy initiatives that not only define Trump as the anti-Obama, but also as more Reaganesque than a "Never Trumper" could ever have imagined. How else to describe a president willing to buck the status quo, and a powerful establishment press, in pulling the U.S. out of the Paris Climate Accords and now refusing to recertify a notoriously deficient nuclear deal with the mullahs in Tehran?

As expected, these decisions have propelled the left (and numerous feckless allies) into yet additional anti-Trump tirades. But this president seems more intent on serving America's long-term interests than attempting to curry favor with a hostile media or spiking his approval numbers in foreign countries. (That even President Obama never dared submit either agreement to Congress in the form of a treaty provides insight into how viable he viewed the respective agreements, but I digress....)

Trump's aggressive contrariness is not confined to foreign policy initiatives. Witness his insistence on a return to the rule of law with respect both to DACA (undocumented children brought to the U.S. at a young age) and Obamacare. Here, the layman executive manifests a better understanding of executive restraint than his constitutional law professor successor. How refreshing, and old-school, to find an administration intending to operate within established constitutional constraints. How stunning to see a president disinclined to unilateral executive action even when the stakes are extraordinarily high.

In this context, Trump has refused to bless an edict rendering millions of undocumented aliens suddenly legal (preferring instead to include relief for DACA children with a comprehensive reform of our broken immigration system), or perpetuate the notion that his Department of Health and Human Services possesses the constitutional authority to hand out taxpayer subsidies to insurance companies when the money has never been appropriated by Congress (preferring instead to maximize consumer choice within a law that has limited too many consumers to a one-size-fits-all menu).

A couple of takeaways present themselves.

Trump is without question a polarizing political figure. It is not difficult to understand how many Americans have deeply held concerns about a revolving-door West Wing and daily policy pronouncements on Twitter. Americans could stand less self-induced drama surrounding the ways and means of the most powerful person in the world.

But there is a seriously refreshing aspect to a leader who understands his job is not to go along to get along, or simply kick the proverbial (policy) cans down the road, but rather to further the economic and national security interests of America first, mainstream media disapproval notwithstanding.

Both Trump and the Resistance Are Doubling Down on Ugly

November 1, 2017, *Washington Examiner*

"Ugly" requires no definition. You know it when you see it. And the public sees plenty of it in what promises to be a four-year war between President Trump and the "Resistance." A related concept is "winning ugly." In sports lexicon, it typically refers to a player or team that competes in unconventional, plodding ways but tends to end up on the winning side.

Both descriptions are appropriate fits as the latest chapters of what I'll call "Russiagate," "Obamacaregate," "tax-reformgate," and "NFLgate" unfold. To wit:

- The Clinton campaign and the Democratic National Committee are now shown to be complicit in the buying and marketing of the now infamous Trump Dossier, while a newly un-muzzled former FBI informant will soon testify about Bill and Hillary's involvement in the Russian purchase of 20 percent of America's uranium reserve.

- Democrats unwilling to negotiate desperately-needed revisions to Obamacare's failing provider networks are lashing out at Trump's hardball tactics of holding up insurer subsidies for poor participants with an eye toward a more comprehensive, "mandate-lite" approach to (partial) repeal and replace.

- Headlines feature brutal GOP internal fractures on the nuts and bolts of tax reform while two (retiring) Republican senators (Jeff Flake and Bob Corker) denounce the ways of the Republican president, who tweets back at them with equal antagonism.

But ugly is not the only description of these high-profile fights. Each also reflects a strong Trump imprint. This president engages and expects to win, with little regard for hurt feelings or broken furniture. That Trump's threats, rants, and innuendo also serve to set Democrats and some establishment Republicans into fits of rage (and overreaction) is now a required addendum to the storyline. Witness the endless headlines devoted to real and imagined Trump misdeeds by the "Never Trump" cable networks. The old adage "it takes two to tango" applies: Both the president and the Resistance never fail to double down on ugly in response to the latest perceived outrage from the other.

And so, it proceeds. The progressive left's fear and loathing daily reaches new lows (or highs depending on one's point of view) every time Trump proves himself the anti-Obama. The mainstream media follow along, often clinging to discredited storylines.

Note that such media "reporting" shares a commonality with the politically correct thought police now appearing on a college campus near you. It is said that this movement rationalizes its hypocrisy by claiming it must renounce its free speech soul in order to achieve a greater good—the defeat of the forces of "-ism," such as capitalism, pluralism, racism, sexism, nationalism, etc. Then and only then can it reconfigure its former self. This act of self-delusion is similar to the media types who knowingly misrepresent and selectively choose what's news, but only in the greater cause of ridding the country of Trump and his deplorables.

Two additional points about all the ugliness must be noted.

The first concerns the president's tendency to oversell—an attribute of a long and generally successful sales career. It is here where overused superlatives are regularly employed: "great," "tremendous," "beautiful," "wonderful"—descriptions that are sometimes disproportionate and often ridiculed. Tweets containing misstatements of fact are yet another legitimate basis for criticism—although it is becoming a common mistake for opponents to overreact to a one day's tweet that is subsequently overridden by a next-day tweet.

The second point is more subtle. It concerns an unintended audience. While ugly narratives feed the Resistance and Trump haters of all stripes, they also tend to drive a subset of lukewarm Trump supporters further to Trump world. The syndrome is familiar. Soft supporters become hardened in the face of relentless ugly because that imperfect guy is still our guy.

Whether the constituent elements of the Resistance truly care about this phenomenon is difficult to gauge. It just may be the antipathy toward anything and everything Trump is so overwhelming that the opposition does not care about losing this (smaller) cohort of voters.

Perhaps they should. After all, these are the soft party identifiers who twice voted for Barack Obama, but were driven by slow economic growth and animus toward Hillary Clinton to the most unlikely of alternatives. These good folks do not necessarily appreciate Trump's own in-artful, sometimes ugly ways. But I kind of think they see a roaring stock market and three percent growth as more akin to winning ugly.

CHAPTER 3

More Jobs...More Growth...
More Happiness

A new federalism has taken hold in Washington. The framers would not recognize it, although many (especially Jefferson) predicted it would unfold. Its focus is the mega-bill: Thousand-plus-page offerings of often arcane language that expand federal jurisdiction and contain numerous fill-in-the-blank provisions that are made the subject of subsequent rulemaking. The structure is a major win for big-government types from both parties. Think about it. The sponsors are happy to proclaim a huge new governmental initiative with accompanying fanfare ("No Child Left Behind," "Dodd-Frank," "The Affordable Care Act"). Supportive constituencies heap praise (and campaign cash) on the bill's cosponsors. These beneficiaries in turn become permanent supporters—and protectors—of the *new* status quo. And unelected federal bureaucrats get to define and expand upon what Congress really meant for the rest of us.

That the Obama administration took full advantage of this bureaucratic construction is a matter of public record. Those blanks were happily filled in by Washington's army of regulators. In the process, the self-proclaimed environmental president killed many thousands of trees—to the ultimate benefit of his regulatory state. The Obama-era onslaught was intense and consistent. According to the Competitive Enterprise Institute, Mr. Obama is the only president to surpass 80,000 pages in the Federal Registry (which includes new federal rules, regulations, and executive orders)—a mark he achieved four times. To boot, seven of the all-time ten highest Federal Register page counts occurred during Obama's eight-year tenure. Seems he really only did need a pen and a phone!

This vastly expanded regulatory authority was the fuel for Mr. Obama's two-term executive power grab. Damage estimates from the assault varied as Republicans assumed full control of the 115th Congress. But House Majority Leader Kevin McCarthy framed the issue succinctly in a January 24, 2017, article for *The Wall Street Journal*:

How the House Will Roll Back Washington's Rule by Bureaucrat

When President Trump delivered his inaugural address last week, he declared that "we are transferring power from Washington, DC, and giving it back to you, the people." Note that he said we are transferring power, in the present tense. The House has already begun turning the president's words into reality by targeting the part of Washington that poses the greatest threat to America's people, economy and Constitution: the federal bureaucracy.

Washington's many agencies, bureaus and departments propagate rules that weigh down businesses, destroy jobs, and limit American freedoms. Career bureaucrats who never face the voters wield punishing authority with little to no accountability. If there's a swamp in Washington, this is it.

In President Obama's final year the Federal Register hit 97,110 pages—longer by nearly 18,000 pages, or 15 King James Bibles, than in 2008. Federal regulations cost the American people about $1.89 trillion every year, according to an estimate by the Competitive Enterprise Institute. That's more than 10 percent of GDP, or roughly $15,000 per American household. The Obama administration has also burdened the public with nearly 583 million hours of compliance over the past eight years, according to the American Action Forum. That's averages to nearly five hours of paperwork for every full-time employee in the country....

Of course, the opaque nature of rulemaking makes it highly effective. It's tough to complain when the damage is unknown or indirect. Here, the calculation of associated expenses is less transparent—but nevertheless quite real for the bottom line of America's job creators.

But elections can change things in a hurry. A businessman replaced a community organizer. Public-sector accountability was suddenly back in style. Two early executive orders set a very different tone: One required federal agencies to eliminate two existing rules for every new one; the other directed regulators to examine financial regulations to determine how they comport with Trump-era efficiencies, including their effectiveness in preventing taxpayer bailouts. Leader McCarthy and his colleagues would be empowered to enact additional structural reforms while utilizing the Congressional Review Act (CRA) to repeal many of the job-killing regulations issued by Obama's agencies during the waning hours of his administration. (Thirteen major Obama regs bit the dust during Trump's first one hundred days.) And what a weapon the CRA is. Few outside of Washington, DC, realize that a recalled regulation under the statute stays dead; subsequent administrations are forbidden from reestablishing the original rule!

An overly aggressive regulatory regime often leads to despotic supervision—and harsh penalties. Two views predominate: An Obama-like heavy-handedness wherein the regulator assumes the role of prosecutor, or the partner model wherein private entities and government seek cooperation for the greater good. The former generates fines, litigation, dollars, and headlines; the latter efficiencies, jobs, and profits. The arrival of the Trump administration signaled a major turn toward option "B." A historic stock market surge and increased consumer confidence offered support for the notion that a tax cut and reduced regulation would spark a revival of the American jobs–producing machine.

The rise, and hoped-for reeling in, of an abusive regulatory state is chronicled in the following columns.

Kitzhaber and How the Left Cooks the Books

February 17, 2015, *National Review*

How we feel about economic development is no substitute for honest analysis.

The resignation last week of Oregon's Governor John Kitzhaber was big news. Big, but not terribly surprising. The Oregon attorney general's office had previously opened an investigation into allegations that the state's first lady, Cylvia Hayes, had improperly utilized state employees in the implementation of a new state metrics policy while she was being paid by an outside group. In the end, Kitzhaber could not stem mounting criticism of his fiancée's dual roles as a gubernatorial adviser and a paid consultant with business before the state—both roles being well-known to the four-term governor.

Alas, today's social media–driven news cycle will move on to the "next big story" in short order. But there is another aspect to this story worth our attention.

You see, the genesis of Governor Kitzhaber's problems lies in Oregon's decision to adopt the so-called Genuine Progress Indicator (GPI), an alternative economic and social-welfare metric that is in various stages of review or implementation in five of America's most liberal states (Vermont, Washington, Hawaii, and Maryland are the others), and which was the project Ms. Hayes had been paid to help manage in Oregon.

GPI's alternative analysis uses twenty-six indicators (divided into economic, environmental, and social) to measure a jurisdiction's overall "health." The individual metrics used will come as no surprise to those who study the progressive playbook: Income inequality, carbon footprint, resource depletion, and CO_2 emissions are prominent economic/environmental indicators. On the social side, costs that are impossible to measure—including positive or negative values of housework, volunteer work, leisure time, and automobile dependency—are included in the index. Such "soft measures" are indeed convenient to those who wish to distance themselves from objective, value-neutral methodologies (such as gross domestic product) that have long been the mainstay of economic-development science.

GPI is classic liberal snake oil for what ails anti-business states. Such knockoff indexes cannot change the objective facts of high tax rates and wealth flight, but they are designed to delegitimize them through a new and politically correct set of criteria more attuned to how one feels about economic development. The GPI mindset is especially useful in explaining away the effects of ill-conceived public policies on hiring and employment. If you are reminded of the famous White House attempt to explain away Obamacare's destructive impact on job creation by pointing out the advantages of increased leisure time...well, so am I.

In reality, GPI represents nothing other than a convenient instrument for progressives to use in obfuscating poor economic performance. In other words, taxpayer beware whenever liberal politicians tell you they're going to measure what really should matter to you—and why you shouldn't worry that so many of your neighbors have retired to more tax-friendly states.

One of the five GPI states—Maryland—is Exhibit A.

Eight years of unrelenting tax increases (forty in all) and a labor-controlled, oppressive regulatory environment saw jobs, wealth, and corporate headquarters fleeing my state. Maryland's gross domestic product showed zero growth in 2013, ranking forty-ninth in the country. All of which was a bridge too far for even this deepest blue of jurisdictions: Larry Hogan became only the sixth Republican Governor of Maryland in 2014 on a transparently clear promise to "stop the [progressive] bleeding."

Now, I'm just as interested in recycling programs, avoiding traffic congestion, and leisure time as the next guy. (Indeed, I would put my environmental record up against any one of my Democratic predecessors.) But I just don't see how soft, non-objective criteria help policy-makers understand what ails job creation. Phrased another way: Hard data are much more valuable than soft in attempting to figure out why your twenty-six-year-old is living in your basement and not on a private-sector payroll.

It is ironic that a government program meant to instill progressive values in Oregon amounts to crony capitalism. If you find yourself living in one of the above-mentioned states and have come to the same conclusion, you might send an email to your governor with the news that you have found a new way to save tax dollars: Try ending feel-good programs that tell us nothing and paper over real problems. Maybe, just maybe, we can return old-fashioned common sense to state government—our feelings notwithstanding.

IRS Plays Fast and Loose with State Migration Data

April 8, 2015, *Washington Examiner*

Think of the statistics our government keeps and publishes—the unemployment rate, the consumer price index, or the gross domestic product. Would these numbers be useful to markets, policymakers, or anyone else concerned about our nation's economic performance if they were released whenever government officials felt like it?

The answer is obviously no.

That is why most government departments and agencies release economic indicators according to a schedule that allows everyone—from Federal Reserve Board governors to county managers—to use data consistently in forming policy.

Unfortunately, that is not the case with a key economic indicator put out by the Internal Revenue Service. The IRS tracks changes in the residential tax base, which the agency's Statistics of Income Division uses to show who is coming and going to every state and county in the nation.

Massive shifts in populations and taxable incomes from northern blue states to red states—most notably Florida, Texas, and South Carolina—have been the trend in recent years. Released in sets of tax years, the agency takes individual filers' tax return addresses and checks to see if and where they moved.

These are more than abstract numbers of interest to think tanks and demographers. They help explain why the twenty-six-year-old living in his or her parents' basement and not independently on a private-sector payroll might be headed far away to find work. According to a Gallup survey on why people move, the ability to find work, taxes, and cost of living are cited as main factors.

Interpreting the most recent data last year, the *Washington Examiner*'s Michael Barone wrote that "there is a large migration away from high-tax states to low-tax states," and a resulting wealth transfer of $7 billion among just six jurisdictions. The bottom line: State tax policy matters.

The problem is the IRS can't seem to figure out when or even whether to release tax migration numbers. In 2012, the IRS publicly cancelled the program, but weeks later reversed themselves after media outlets (including the *Washington Examiner*) called attention to it.

Tax Foundation economist Joseph Henchman applauded the agency for continuing the program, adding an important caveat: "I'm immensely curious as to who ordered them to cancel it in the first place, and why."

So are a lot of others, including myself. As a former governor from a blue state, I heard anecdotal evidence for years about people fleeing Maryland to surrounding states and along the I-95 corridor to Virginia, the Carolinas, and on to Florida. On recent trips to Florida, which has no income tax, I have asked people to raise their hands if they are from Maryland, which happens so often it is not a surprise anymore.

In a widely publicized finding, Maryland lost over 31,000 people and $1.7 billion in taxable incomes to other states between 2007 and 2010. Stemming tax flight and lowering the tax burden became a key plank in the GOP gubernatorial campaigns of Larry Hogan in Maryland, Bruce Rauner in Illinois, and Charlie Baker in Massachusetts. These successful candidates proved that decisions in state capitols affect the lives of voters.

Fast-forward to today. The IRS is now releasing data so late, and in such a haphazard manner, that it is becoming useless. As most of us are ready to file tax returns for 2014, the IRS will be releasing migration data for tax years 2011 and 2012 in July. This came just days after the agency said they would be released in "the fall." Last year, the most recent numbers (for 2010 and 2011) were released in April.

Confused? So am I.

Fearing Congressional scrutiny, negative press attention, or the outright cancelation of the program, perhaps the IRS now prefers to sweep the program under the rug. Yet most rational taxpayers would probably like to weigh the consequences of tax policy on economic growth in their states rather than see the entire issue devolve into partisan politics.

The IRS has lost a lot of credibility during the Obama administration. Putting out tax migration data in a consistent, timely manner like other economic statistics is an opportunity to get a little of it back.

The Next Repeal and Replace: Dodd-Frank

January 28, 2017, *Forbes*

Note: This post was coauthored by J. C. Boggs.

DISCLOSURE: The authors are members of the government advocacy and public policy team at King & Spalding, where their clients include financial services companies that could benefit from a repeal and replace of Dodd-Frank.

The Wall Street Reform and Consumer Protection Act of 2010, better known as "Dodd-Frank," was constructed hastily and upon poor foundations that will require significant structural alterations. Fortunately, help is on the way. President Trump supports dismantling Dodd-Frank for the simple reason that "banks aren't lending money to people who need it." Not only has Dodd-Frank restricted overall loan making by banks, it has made it more difficult for marginally creditworthy smaller businesses and consumers to secure favorably priced loans. A recent University of Maryland study found that because of Dodd-Frank, "lenders reduced credit to middle-class households by 15 percent, and increased credit to wealthy households by 21 percent."

Under Dodd-Frank, all bank holding companies with consolidated assets of more than $50 billion were automatically designated as "too big to fail." The irony is that Dodd-Frank's focus on "too big to fail" created a new problem—"too small to succeed"—as complex and costly regulations required small banks to hire compliance officers instead of lending officers.

Today, the five biggest banks control 44 percent of all U.S. banking assets—more than before Dodd-Frank was enacted. At the same time, more than 1,700 small and community banks—nearly one-quarter of the industry—have been forced to merge or shut down.

With Dodd-Frank, Congress rewrote 140 years of banking law, going back to the National Bank Act of 1864, in just fourteen months. During our respective tenures as a Member of Congress and Senate Banking Committee counsel, we have never witnessed such audacity. But that was just the tip of the iceberg.

In an unprecedented delegation of authority to federal regulators, the legislation resulted in the promulgation of approximately 24,000 pages of new regulation. Six years after enactment, only 70 percent of the nearly 400 regulations required by the act have been finalized, 10 percent are pending, and 20 percent have yet to be proposed.

Nowhere is such regulatory abuse more obvious than the so-called "Volcker Rule" prohibiting banks and their affiliates from trading securities for their own account, although Democratic bill drafters could produce no evidence that proprietary trading contributed to the 2008 financial crisis. To make matters worse, a recent Federal Reserve staff working paper concluded that the net effect of the Volcker Rule is a less liquid corporate bond market.

Equally problematic, the new Financial Stability Oversight Council (FSOC) was given the extraordinary power to designate non-bank financial firms as "systemically important financial institutions." While traditional insurance activities played no role in the financial crisis and pose no risk to the financial system, these non-bank "SIFIs" are now subject to increased capital and regulatory requirements, whose costs are ultimately being borne by the consumer.

Dodd-Frank also created the Consumer Financial Protection Bureau (CFPB), a $600 million annual behemoth generating more than $5 billion in fines since its inception. The CFPB is funded by the Federal Reserve, evading our constitutional structure in which Congress appropriates funds for executive-branch operations. Its rulemaking is equally out of control with one regulation on mortgage lending exceeding 1,000 pages.

While Dodd-Frank is the primary villain here, associated legal risk remains a factor. Banks hit with legal settlements in the billions because of subprime mortgages also were forced by government agencies to repurchase loans. The end result—the slow recovery and one of the lowest growth periods in our nation's history.

Innovation is another casualty. Smaller banks, in particular, complain that new rules and regulations limit the types of products and services they can offer. The result has been to drive much of today's financial innovation to non-bank companies outside of the regulated rails, and often outside the United States. To compound matters, the FDIC has approved only three new bank charters since 2010, by far the lowest approval rate in our nation's history.

Fortunately, a market-based alternative in the form of the Financial CHOICE Act has been introduced by House Financial Services Committee Chairman Jeb Hensarling and passed by the U.S. House of Representatives this past September. The CHOICE Act would allow banks to raise their leverage ratio to ten percent in exchange for freedom from Dodd-Frank regulation. Further, the FSOC could no longer designate SIFI status to non-banks, thereby subjecting them to more bank-like regulation.

The Hensarling bill also turns the CFPB into a bipartisan commission, funded by Congress per constitutional requirements. The proposal would also mandate that all new financial regulations pass a cost-benefit test prior to implementation.

Senate procedure generally requires sixty votes to pass legislation, and there are just fifty-two Republican Senators who would presumably support a rollback of Dodd-Frank. Republicans will need at least eight Democrats to get the job done. Alternatively, the GOP could tie the bill, or at least parts of it, to budget reconciliation, which would allow them to make legislative changes with a simple majority.

A market-oriented majority and pro-business president can lead the way to a less costly landscape for small banks—and renewed hope for small businesses and startups with the credit they've needed but lacked under Dodd-Frank. Time to get moving again!

Not Your Father's NLRB

October 13, 2016, *Washington Examiner*

All of us are familiar with the history of FDR and the bedrock elements of his New Deal coalition. Recently arrived immigrants, blacks, and urban blue-collar whites gave Roosevelt their votes and their steadfast devotion on the electoral path to four consecutive wins.

But the foundation of this powerful coalition was organized labor—a gritty generation of working-class Democrats who would remain faithful to the Democratic Party's brand until a steady move left in the 1960s began to strain what had been a spectacularly successful relationship.

Indeed, beginning with George McGovern and proceeding to the present day, private-sector union members have continued to migrate toward the GOP in national elections—so much so that union-dominated Rust Belt states are now an essential component for a Donald Trump (or, for that matter, any GOP nominee) victory in a presidential election cycle.

But big labor's leadership has not followed suit. Their relentless efforts to expand membership rolls—a long-term losing proposition—require a steadfast commitment to the Democratic ticket, their members' wishes (and especially their social views) notwithstanding.

This history sets the stage for an under-the-radar yet hugely significant issue in this highly charged election season. I refer to the makeup of the National Labor Relations Board (NLRB), that powerful group of individuals tasked with the job of calling balls and strikes in the modern workplace. Their decisions carry immense impact on union organizing activities—and the private-sector job creators who must abide by NLRB decisions.

Few would argue that the Obama era has turned the NLRB into a decidedly labor-left direction. Three of its most notorious decisions come easily to mind.

There was an egregious 2011 charge of illegal retaliation against Washington-based Boeing for its decision to open a new factory in right-to-work South Carolina. Note that no Washington-based union member lost a job as a result of the move. Nevertheless, Boeing decided to settle the complaint. Few private-sector employees failed to notice the dangerous precedent.

There was President Obama's attempt to make three recess appointments in January of 2012—despite the fact that the Senate was not in recess at the time. Alas, a 2014 Supreme Court decision nullifying the appointments was partially undone when a Republican Senate agreed to approve a slate of new pro-labor nominees.

Then there was the recent decision to charge McDonald's as a "joint employer" with its franchises for purposes of litigating unfair labor practice complaints. This despite the fact that the vast majority of McDonald's restaurants (80 percent) are independently owned and operated.

(For a more thorough analysis, see *Washington Examiner* columnist Sean Higgins's column of September 12, 2016, "How Obama Has Titled the Workplace for Unions.")

Note that while there does appear to be an outer limit to the board's seemingly endless quest to expand organizing rights (a full board overturned a regional office's decision that Northwestern University's football team could unionize), the fact remains that the Obama NLRB has morphed into a game-changing subsidiary of organized labor. And nobody in Washington, DC, believes Hillary Clinton will do anything to change the status quo.

The advent of this decidedly anti-employer majority has coincided with the weakest economic recovery in fifty years. More recently, it has coincided with the rise of Trump. Most political pundits tie Trump's rise to the federal government's perceived indifference to the enforcement of our immigration laws and the serial failures of the GOP Congressional leadership to confront a wildly progressive president.

There is some truth to the theory, but the primary cause of the Trump phenomenon is Obama-era slow growth—that unsustainable 1–2 percent per year growth rate that has choked so many working-class households and given rise to a well-chronicled sense of hopelessness in blue-collar America.

This working-class discontent has further stressed what remains of the Democratic Party's hold on white, blue-collar union members. These folks still work with their hands. Some envision starting a business of their own. They reject Obama's "you didn't build that" mantra. And they do not resent wealth or "the 1 percent"; they simply want an opportunity to give their children a better life—the essential definition of the "American dream."

How ironic that the union households that flock to Trump rallies by the tens of thousands are the same workers a rabidly progressive union leadership and NLRB majority claim to represent.

What Do Burgers, Fries, and Economic Growth Have to Do with Each Other?

June 19, 2017, *Washington Examiner*

A few weeks ago, I wrote about a number of the less-publicized but nevertheless important policy changes brought about by the Trump administration. These initiatives are not the stuff of bold headlines but rather sector-specific injunctions that have serious impact on job creation and economic growth.

The list of such hoped-for policy reversals is indeed long, but rational partisans understand that even "to-do lists" must be prioritized in a slow-moving body such as Congress. The question then becomes which Obama-era policies are causing the most damage to job producers and what is the most efficient way to remedy the situation?

One issue that fits the bill is the Obama National Labor Relations Board's not-so-improved definition of "joint employer"—what was a term of art in labor law until a progressive board majority saw an opportunity to feed its labor boss constituency.

The dirty deed was accomplished by changing the definition of employer from those exercising direct workplace control over employees to those having "indirect" or "reserved" control. Such an extraordinary definitional stretch subjects employers to increased liability for the actions of "employees" they have neither hired nor exercised control over. Another intended byproduct is more dues-paying worker bees pumping ever more money into union coffers—and more campaign contributions out the door to their Democratic Party beneficiaries.

For those not practiced in the language of labor law, think of your local McDonald's, Wendy's, Burger King, Arby's. The vast majority of these businesses are franchises owned and operated by entrepreneurs subject to a franchise agreement. (A few "company stores" retain company ownership.) The franchise owner manages and runs the operation, including employment decisions with respect to hiring and firing.

One impact of the NLRB's decision has been to freeze engagement of new franchisees. Fewer locations means fewer jobs and less growth, but franchisors simply do not need the headache of being held legally responsible for employees they do not control.

There are two primary reasons this change of policy has hit home in the small business world, where 85 percent of new jobs are produced.

First is the reality of overturning thirty years' worth of clearly established law—not such a big deal to progressives engaged in the act of transforming the country, especially the modern workplace, but a very big deal to corporations that wish to expand through a franchise model and aspiring franchisees who dream of owning their own business.

Second, it was the small business community and the people they employ that defined the Trump "movement"—a political coalition borne of the Obama era's slow economic growth whose members registered historic turnout in Rust Belt states on Election Day. You can still see them from time to time on your television screen at continuing Trump "campaign" rallies. They are the ones wearing the red "Make America Great Again" hats. They are also the ones worried that economic stagnation through overregulation and overtaxation is killing the working class.

Herein is a clash of major political players during a time of sustained inadequate growth. On the one hand is a progressive NLRB in cahoots with organized labor seeking to amend a principle of labor law universally accepted over the last thirty years in order to generate new paying members (and increase employer legal exposure) during a time private-sector union membership continues to suffer a precipitous decline. On the other side of the aisle are small businesses weary after eight long years of playing defense as an Obama-controlled

NLRB majority did its best to enact organized labor's agenda through administrative fiat (a game effort that was only slowed down by periodic adverse court decisions).

But that was then. President Trump's Labor Secretary Alexander Acosta has now withdrawn an Obama-era "guidance document" that expanded employer liability. This decision will assuredly be followed by additional moves to reverse Obama-era overreach. A conservative, small business–friendly GOP Congressional majority stands ready to assist, as does President Trump, whose entire presidency rides on his ability to kick-start the job creation machine into the neighborhood of 3 percent annual growth.

Present and prospective employers and employees have much at stake. Numerous bills and appropriations riders have been introduced in both chambers of Congress in order to remedy this egregious decision. For now, the DOL's guidance recall is a significant first step in the right direction. But Congress needs to follow suit—and soon.

In the Age of Trump, Populism Ain't What It Used to Be

August 11, 2017, *Washington Examiner*

Populism is a term easily thrown around in today's political lexicon. But it is often misapplied.

American-style populism dates to the era of William Jennings Bryan at the end of the nineteenth century. Bryan's movement was a protest against Wall Street greed and the big banks. Rhetorical warfare in opposition to the ways and means of the upper classes was the fuel; "free silver" (in order to drive up commodity prices) and trustbusting became its preferred goals. The anti-wealth flavor of this easily agitated faction continues to be recognizable among today's leading Democrats.

Now fast-forward to a New York real estate tycoon and recently elected president and his program to kick-start economic growth. Fully half of the Trump economic agenda is traditional, Reaganesque economics—cutting business and personal taxes, regulatory retrenchment, tort reform. This is familiar policy right out of the Republican playbook. But the other half of the program reflects a truly populist rift targeted to the voters who got President Trump elected last November—alienated working-class folks who feel betrayed by the Washington establishment and left behind in an era of increasing globalism.

Trump's distaste for omnibus trade deals and a ballooning trade deficit was established early during the 2016 campaign. Recall candidate Trump targeting "unfair" trade agreements as a major contributing factor to a declining Rust Belt economy. Accordingly, one of Trump's very first acts was to disengage the U.S. from the Trans Pacific Partnership. This single act has become a key talking point at Trump post-election campaign rallies around the country, to sustained applause.

The paradigm shift is dramatic. Gone are the days of extended multiparty negotiations. America's trade representatives now look to negotiate bilateral agreements—a slower and cumbersome track, but one where economic impact is more easily calibrated for those who wish to keep score.

Voters should take note that even where it will be difficult to leave an existing trade agreement (i.e., NAFTA), the administration will insist on modernizing amendments and new side agreements intended to assist U.S. exporters. You can bet every new surplus (or improving deficit) with a trading partner will be duly noted at future campaign rallies.

But the most visible element of Trump populism concerns immigration—illegal and legal. The former defined candidate Trump. He would build that "big, beautiful wall" and get Mexico to pay for it. He would bolster the disillusioned border patrol. He would use his bully pulpit to send a message that the new sheriff in town means business.

Eight months later, it appears the message has hit home. Illegal border crossings have fallen to seventeen-year lows, prior to construction of the wall or the passage of a comprehensive immigration bill.

The president's plan for legal immigration has now assumed center stage with his recent endorsement of a Senate reform bill that makes marketable skills a higher immigration priority and seeks to limit the overall number of new immigrants. Both goals comport with Trump's political and substantive indictment of the immigration status quo, but each contravenes long-established GOP policy.

Talk about an awkward juxtaposition. Trump's approach is contrary to what big business and the GOP leadership have preached for the last three decades—even Ronald Reagan supported increased levels of legal immigration (and cut an amnesty deal regarding illegals). But Trump's targeted audience is not the Chamber of Commerce or the socially conservative groups that have supported liberalized immigration in the interest of keeping families intact. This president's focus is Main Street USA, a place where plenty of voters believe the influx of cheap labor has contributed to the loss of lower-skilled manufacturing jobs.

A fascinating sidelight here concerns those organized interests who are not a part of this populist uprising but should be. I refer to minorities and organized labor. Here, basic economics should lead both groups to oppose the over-supply of cheap labor that keeps wages depressed and marginal American families...marginal.

But this is the age of Trump and strident partisan conflict. The NAACP and (most) big labor bosses have long jettisoned economic sense for politics—Democratic politics, that is. The Trump administration should expect no help from either group in its campaign to limit legal or illegal immigration.

Another interesting element here concerns how the president will integrate recent strong economic indicators (labor participation is way up, as are job openings) with his plans for limiting legal immigration and a smaller labor pool. My prediction: Trump will not abandon his economic populism even as he takes credit for a booming stock market and historically low unemployment. After all, past recoveries and periodic bouts of solid growth have bypassed his targeted Rust Belt audience.

This time, they will not be forgotten.

CHAPTER 4

The Unnatural Disaster Known as Obamacare: Finding a Successor

It was Barack Obama's signature piece of legislation. Finally, the federal government would guarantee universal health insurance coverage—a long promised goal of the Democratic Party. But what began as a dysfunctional website never got much better. Along the way, it was at least partially responsible for the loss of over 1,000 Democratic seats at all levels of government.

The embarrassingly misnamed Affordable Care Act ("Obamacare") proved to be a predictable disaster—various degrees of negligence permeated its construction and subsequent path throughout the legislative process. The passing of a liberal icon also played a part. Scott Brown's upset victory in Massachusetts after the death of Senator Edward Kennedy meant that Democrats would be denied their sixty-vote filibuster-proof majority in the U.S. Senate. Hence, Majority Leader Harry Reid would be forced to use extraordinary procedural mechanisms to secure passage of the legislation that few members had read—and even fewer understood.

At its core, Obamacare will be best remembered for its failure to deliver on President Obama's two most infamous and serially repeated promise(s): 1) You can keep your insurance and your doctor, and 2) the average family will save $2,500 per year in health care expenditures. Alas, these empty, foundational assurances are rarely if ever noted by today's Obama apologists—and *never* by the former president in his many post-presidential Facebook posts.

That Obamacare succeeded in increasing Medicaid rolls by seven million enrollees is a matter of fact. Thirty-two (mostly Democrat) governors took the federal government's "free" money in order to expand their rolls. But all of this begs the question: Why didn't Mr. Obama seek to simply expand this entitlement as a stand-alone measure rather than disrupt the larger health care marketplace with a complex anti-market monster chock-full of perverse incentives?

Many critical pieces have been written about Obamacare, but three prominent pre-Trump storylines stand out in the brief, tortured history of the legislation. These include the public relations disaster that accompanied the original Obamacare exchange–related computer glitches; Professor Jonathan Gruber's embarrassing, after-the-fact comments regarding the multiple manipulations he perpetrated in order to create his Frankenstein; and the miserable timing of Obamacare-inspired premium hikes that hit hard in middle-class America on the eve of the 2016 general election—and in turn cast a dark cloud over Hillary Clinton's abiding support for the largely unpopular law.

Post-election polling reflects what many Republicans had banked on: Obamacare's myriad shortcomings played a direct role in Mrs. Clinton's electoral downfall. Middle-class voters were unhappy about Obamacare's taxes, premium increases, limited networks, high deductibles, and coverage mandates. The continuing dysfunction of Mr. Obama's signature piece of legislation only strengthened voter disgust with Washington's incompetence.

As for the Republicans and Trump, "repeal and replace" was the go-to campaign mantra—a winning and easy stump strategy in venues full of partisans accustomed to badmouthing Obamacare's seemingly endless shortcomings. But as the post-election debate began, the GOP was well aware that the rhetoric now required definition. The majority also knew that two Obamacare provisions remained popular: a pre-existing condition prohibition and coverage requirements until age twenty-six. These and other mandates would prove problematic for drafters determined to repair broken insurance markets. Further complications would arise from a GOP determination to place the brakes on a Medicaid entitlement that had metastasized far beyond its original charter. Alas, few were surprised when the House Republican leadership's initial attempt at "replace" was met with such furious bipartisan opposition that the bill was pulled from floor consideration. An overly confident House leadership had whiffed in its first real test.

What to do next was not clear. An alternative strategy acceptable to all wings of the party was not readily apparent. A major opportunity to lead had been lost, and a rare setback for a newly installed president set the GOP on its heels. Nevertheless, Republicans (at least *House* Republicans) well understood a replacement was a "must pass" if the party desired to maintain its Congressional majorities. And this the House finally succeeded in by a skinny margin of 217–213 votes shortly after the administration had celebrated its "First Hundred Days." Yet no such magical results could be replicated on the other side of the Capitol as Senate Republicans did not just swing and miss—they struck out in the bottom of the ninth. In response, a frustrated president threatened to let Obamacare wither on the vine. The GOP Senate was fresh out of ideas, and the difficulties in securing a Senate majority were compounded by the president's low ratings in public opinion polls.

In the meantime, the Democrats continue to do what they do best—protect entitlements at all costs. Their desperate attempts to save Obama's Medicaid legacy sound the familiar refrain that "[fill in the blank] million people will lose their health care" if Republicans repeal Obamacare. Such is the oft-repeated media indictment—a narrative that has put the fear of God into GOP moderates.

The hyperaggressive Mr. Trump would refuse to take GOP inaction for an answer. Statutory reform had become comatose. But the never-say-die president had a less complicated alternative in mind: executive action. An end to cost sharing subsidies paid to insurers in order to offset discounts provided to low income subscribers and the approval of "mandate lite," less expensive plans were the initial modifications offered by a president intent on unwinding as much of Obamacare's infrastructure as possible.

Going forward, remedial actions would take the form of more narrow executive branch tweaks or (more unlikely) statutory changes that could muster 50 Senate votes. As for comprehensive repeal and replace, the following articles critique what has gone wrong so far—and why.

P.S. Obamacare: Five Years Later

August 18, 2016, *Washington Examiner*

On occasion, a single piece of legislation captures the essence of a political movement. Such is the case with the Affordable Care Act, aka "Obamacare," the signature piece of Obama-era legislation now in its sixth year.

Passage of the historic bill marked the high point of progressive power, fueled by a Democratic president and Democratic control of both Houses of Congress. Though this full-court press could not deliver the ultimate goal—single-payer government-run health care—the next best thing was offered as a sound intermediate step. Here, Hillary Clinton's (circa 1993) much maligned health care reform had come full circle—even if Speaker Nancy Pelosi could not quite describe the constituent elements of the bill. But, no matter—the content was deemed far less important than the fact of passage: "[We] have to pass the bill so that you [the people] can find out what's in it."

Enough time has passed for most Americans to "find out what's in" the overhyped and underdelivering law. In other words, what do we know now that we did not know then?

Professor Jonathan Gruber, the architect of Obamacare, deliberately disassembled Obamacare's fiscal impact to encourage the Congressional Budget Office (CBO) to produce a desperately needed "deficit-neutral" report on the bill. We know this because the good professor admitted as much in a recorded, after-the-fact panel discussion wherein he bragged that the "tortured" way the bill was written was "to make sure the CBO did not score the mandate as taxes [which would have ensured] the bill dies." Such manipulation was mandatory; the bill *had* to pass. Postscript: The taxpayers paid Gruber $400,000 for his handiwork.

Nothing gets a progressive more upset than a group of elderly nuns insisting on their religious liberty, hence the Obama administration's Supreme Court battle with the "Little Sisters of the Poor" over Obamacare's "conscience clause" mandate to change their health plan to include contraceptive and reproductive procedures contrary to Catholic doctrine. Mr. Obama's half-hearted attempt to accommodate the Little Sisters has led to a Supreme Court order to negotiate a compromise. Postscript: The "Little Sisters" refused to bend even in the face of multimillion-dollar fines, still a partial win for religious liberty.

More than half of Obamacare's co-ops have failed, costing U.S. taxpayers over $1 billion in government-backed loans. Many pundits predicted just such a result since few experts believed these intended alternative options would attract enough customers to compete against more mature marketplace players. In some cases, state regulators have been required to move fast in order to shut down nonprofitable players so that consumers could shift to other plans prior to year end. Postscript: Twenty-one of the original twenty-three co-ops were underwater at the end of 2015. Postscript #2: Democratic Members of Congress want to further subsidize insurers that lose money on the Obamacare marketplace. Postscript #3: Some things never change.

Arguably, Obamacare's worst provision was the medical device tax, effective January 1, 2013. The levy was solely intended to be a new revenue source for the federal government. It has cost jobs (195,000 direct and indirect jobs, according to a 2015 study by the Advanced Medical Technology Association), slowed job creation, and reduced capital investment. Look at the reduction in research and development as a direct assault on new product creation—the same products that give us higher quality and longer lives. One measure of the tax's dysfunction is that *even Senator Elizabeth Warren supports its* repeal. This bad idea has no fans—other than the outgoing president of the United States.

Obamacare's authors intended to leverage the consolidation of physicians into large practice groups in order to improve health care delivery. This they accomplished as recent hospital mergers have accelerated at a rapid pace. But even some of the law's remaining fans see the flaw in their theory (see Bob Kocher's "mea culpa" in the August 1 edition of *The Wall Street Journal*) as smaller independent physician-led accountable care organizations outperform their larger, consolidated competitors. The reason is not surprising to fans of market competition: Smaller providers are more flexible, innovative, and responsive to consumer (patient) needs. Who would have thought...

"Risk-corridor" payments were created to compensate carriers who lost money on Obamacare exchanges—which explains why some major insurance companies supported Obamacare in the first place. Now comes news of lawsuits filed by major carriers in order to recoup their losses. Recall these dollars were to be collected from carriers who made money on the exchanges. But there is a problem: Few carriers turned a profit *and* Congressional Republicans passed budget language that limits the corridor program to pay out only surplus (profit—no taxpayer subsidies).

Fun Fact #1

In 2014, carriers requested $2.87 billion in risk-corridor payments, but only $362 million came in from profits.

Fun Fact #2

Major players such as Aetna, Anthem, Humana, and UnitedHealth Group are cutting back on their Obamacare participation.

Conclusion

Perverse incentives, cost shifting, increasing deductibles and co-pays, hurtful tax increases, and consumer frustration define Obamacare. It just doesn't work very well—a fact that should be front and center in the fall campaign.

Facts...and Opinions

March 8, 2017, *Washington Examiner*

The long awaited "replace" has arrived. The battle is now joined. A mainstream media wholly invested in the political failure of a replacement to Obamacare will not be helpful.

As the trench warfare begins, it is an appropriate time to review the facts as we know them. It will then be my right as an American citizen (and columnist) to offer an accompanying opinion—for your consumption. Warning: The remainder of this essay may cause depression and severe constipation for progressives continuing to cling to a law they still haven't read, but that now defines them.

Fact #1

Republicans made the last four election cycles a referendum on Obamacare. Each time, Democrats' up- and downballot got hammered. The final Democratic casualty count was 63 House seats, 9 Senate seats, 13 governorships, 524 state legislative seats, and 18 State Chambers.

Opinion

This brutal record of electoral defeat is lost on progressive activists and their enablers in the Democratic leadership. Their attachment to the legislation is unshakeable. Look for renewed street protests and disruptive town halls as the legislative process gets serious this spring.

Fact #2

Three baseline promises were employed by President Barack Obama in taking his case for health care reform to the American public. In no particular order: "You can keep your doctor," "You can keep your health insurance," "You will save an average of $2,500 annually on your health insurance." Each commitment proved untrue. The president's continued use of the "If you like your health plan, you can keep it" line earned him *PolitiFact*'s "2013 Lie of the Year."

Opinion

Few substantive responses have been offered to this devastating line of attack. A typical line begins with a wish the Republicans would have been more cooperative during the first year of the Obama presidency. But it was the president and Democratic leadership who kicked Republicans to the curb on health care reform. No GOP alternatives were entertained. This bit of uncompromising partisanship came back to bite the Democrats in the aftermath of Obamacare's disastrous rollout. Political reminder: Throwing a rope to a drowning opponent is not an option in the absence of demonstrated good faith.

Fact #3

A key player in the drafting of the Affordable Care Act "wrote the bill in a tortured way" (in order to hide its tax burden), all the while "relying on the stupidity of the American voter to sell it."

Opinion

These words from professor Jonathan Gruber reflect the intellectual (dis)honesty of the bill's chief architect. No wonder so many moderate Democrats ran for the hills once all the duplicity came to light. But many could not run fast enough—see FACT #1.

Fact #4

Major insurance carriers continue to exit Obamacare networks for the most basic of reasons: They are unable to make a profit. It gets worse. The federal exchanges continue to lose plans and customers, while only four of the original twenty-four Obamacare co-ops remained in business as of January 1.

Opinion

Hillary Clinton's campaign paid a high price for last fall's announcements regarding Obamacare premium increases. A new round of price hikes this spring will likewise upset the "fix-but-don't-replace" Democrats.

Fact #5

Medicaid was originally passed as a joint state-federal social safety net program for the benefit of poor women with children and people with disabilities. The program experienced incremental growth over the years until Obamacare blew the doors off with a 100 percent federal contribution for new enrollees that is guaranteed to never go lower than 90 percent. Many (not all) governors expanded their eligibility rolls in order to sign up for the "free" federal dollars.

Opinion

That millions of these new Medicaid recipients could have been removed from the program is the foundation for Democratic charges that Republicans will cause poor people to lose their health coverage. But the new draft *postpones* the issue; expansion is funded through 2019 *when things really change.*

Fact #6

The new draft contains a long sought-after GOP objective by block-granting Medicaid—thereby providing states the fiscal resources to serve the poor while allowing for maximum flexibility. The size of individual state grants will be derived from 2016 per recipient spending levels.

Opinion

Maintaining Obamacare levels of spending for an additional three years is intended to mitigate the reality of a truly transformative change beginning in 2020. Some Republicans will oppose the continued spending, while Democrats will oppose the proposed block grants. This is all heavy lifting indeed.

Fact #7

Obama-era Congressional majorities voted to repeal Obamacare in excess of sixty times.

Opinion

Much of the draft contains provisions that have appeared in past repeal bills. This initial proposal repeals the individual and business mandates, and their complex income-based subsidy formulas. These are replaced by a refundable tax credit tied to age and income and targeted to the working poor and working-class folks who make too much money to qualify for Medicaid and are not covered at work. Freedom Caucus types are not excited by the prospect, but Republicans typically utilize tax credits (not just deductions) in order to achieve policy outcomes. The ACA's exchanges survived but will assuredly sink with the absence of taxpayer subsidies. Extremely popular health savings accounts are expanded, and the tax preference for employer-provided health insurance is kept in place. Look for conservatives to revisit the Medicaid compromise and seek to eliminate Obamacare's taxes now rather than next year. Look for Democrats to scream bloody murder.

Second Opinion

All in all, it's a serious step in the right direction.

Obamacare Repeal and Replace Heads Back into the Fire

June 12, 2017, *Washington Examiner*

One of the great lessons in life is to "keep it simple." Yet, the most frequent violators are the people who should understand it best. I refer to the political class, specifically elected officials who (often unsuccessfully) engage needless complexities in lawmaking.

For example, there would be far more Democrats in Washington today if the drafting of Obamacare had not so violated the rule. Indeed, its primary author (Professor Jonathan Gruber) bragged that he made the language far more complex than needed—the better to confuse the opposition and disguise the bill's heavy tax burden.

More recently, it has been Republicans' turn to cross a "simple" divide. As a result, much of the GOP base opposed an Obamacare repeal and replace bill that cut taxes, ended the individual mandate, defunded Planned Parenthood, and block-granted Medicaid.

Talk about a lose-lose. A new GOP president was unable to bring his first major bill to the floor in a Congress controlled by his party, and many of the voters who put him there didn't know whether to be happy or angry. (Most were confused.)

But that storyline is now so February. Speaker of the House Paul Ryan's leadership team used the previous bill as a predicate—then negotiated with enough "gettable" members to secure passage of a new bill, the American Health Care Act, by four votes.

All in all, a positive result. Obamacare will not be allowed to simply wither on the vine. After all, the voters gave Republicans control in major part because Obamacare was dysfunctional. The GOP recipients of this political gift could ill afford to simply walk away as dire times approach. They were hired to fix it.

Going forward, the GOP must honor Rule One.

The AHCA must be artfully communicated. No Obama-like overpromising need occur. In the process, Americans should be reminded that the fracturing of Obamacare's provider networks and the inability of insurance carriers to make a profit are the real reasons the status quo cannot stand. Here, Trump must take the lead in communicating the ways in which his bill is preferable to its failed predecessor—how it will facilitate competition, lower premiums, and improve health care.

A few simple, easily understood planks for your consumption:

Obamacare's taxes are repealed.

The AHCA guts Obamacare's twenty-one new or increased taxes. Total tax relief is estimated to be $992 billion. (Spending is cut by $1.1 trillion.)

Consumer choice is restored.

The preservation of Obamacare's mandates within "Ryancare" required consumers to buy services they did not need at a cost they could not afford. But one-size-fits-all is expensive and hinders innovation. Potential purchasers were not impressed. Carriers suffered huge losses. Today, one-third of subdivisions are down to a single carrier on their Obamacare exchanges while two entire regions of the country have no carriers left. (Aetna and Humana have announced they will forgo participation in all Obamacare exchanges in 2018.) Accordingly, the AHCA allows states to opt out of some mandates, thereby inviting more flexible, cheaper alternatives into the market.

Block-granting Medicaid is a big deal.

Everyone in Washington bemoans the bipartisan lack of interest in reforming entitlements. Recall that Trump promised "hands-off" of entitlements on the campaign trail.

But the AHCA brings real change to a broken Medicaid program by providing states a fixed amount of money per beneficiary and flexibility on how to design their anti-poverty programs. (Such systemic change is already underway in a number of red and blue states operating under previously obtained waivers.) A historic redesign that allows states to move the program closer to its original purpose—subsidizing poor women with children and people with disabilities—is now doable, despite progressive cries of bloody murder regarding "lost" coverage.

Here, note that almost all of those who will see reduced or changed coverage under the AHCA are able-bodied, working-age adults.

Price must reflect risk.

Recall Obama's promise that Obamacare would lower premiums by $2,500 per family.

It failed to do so. Four election cycles later, the voters still have not forgotten.

How could they? New numbers from the Department of Health and Human Services reflect that average premiums in the individual market have increased 105 percent (over the past four years) within federally run Obamacare exchanges.

Prohibitions on pre-existing condition disclaimers is the principal reason. No surprise here. It is difficult for underwriters to make a buck when the law stops them from...underwriting.

But a strong cultural value has emerged: People demand that older, sicker people not be priced out of the health insurance marketplace. Accordingly, the new bill subsidizes risk pools in order to cover more expensive patients in the individual market—a compromise that spreads the social cost of doing the right thing to all taxpayers.

Remaining consumers in that market will now be able to take advantage of more affordable policies as priced by more stable markets.

Lessons learned.

The initial attempt to repeal/replace gave all involved a black eye. The Democrats crowed. A new president fumed. The alphabet soup networks laughed out loud. GOP partisans wondered why seven years was not enough time for the Republican leadership to get its act together. But it was all first-quarter action. It is now the Senate's obligation to keep the offense rolling into the second half.

As a former Member of Congress, I understand Ryan's original approach better than most. Senate rules constitute a real obstacle to a comprehensive repeal and replace. And it's never easy to manage the conflicting demands of the moderates vis-à-vis the conservatives.

But the messaging failed. The GOP's talking points were ineffective.

Once the two chambers do their thing, a conference committee will be appointed. Whatever vehicle emerges will constitute a Republican legacy, up for a de facto referendum in November 2018.

Here's hoping that the GOP takes full advantage of this rare opportunity for a do-over. Only then will the messy memory of "Ryancare I" be put to rest.

Republicans Need to Play Obamacare Repeal Right or Face Disaster in 2018

July 20, 2017, *Washington Examiner*

It's a shame Senate Republicans are having such a difficult time getting their act together on health care. After all, *Obamacare: Reality Sucks* is playing all over the country right now, to dreadful reviews for familiar reasons.

Major carriers continue to flee Obamacare exchanges *en masse*, its co-ops continue to go belly-up (only four of the original twenty-three remain in business), and its networks continue to shrink. Without a massive influx of subsidies, the program's demise is no longer "if," but "when." And our old friend, Professor Jonathan Gruber, is nowhere to be found.

Yet, despite all of this unraveling, recent polls reflect newfound support for the embattled program. The reform that contributed mightily to historic Democratic losses in the House and Senate is suddenly, if not popular, at least not so unpopular.

Alas, the public does not appreciate confusion when it comes to their health care. They understand Obamacare has fatal flaws, but what of the "replace" part of "repeal and replace?" Here, the GOP Senate's bumbling and stumbling is embarrassing; its credibility diminishes by the second.

Meanwhile, Democrats have doubled down on defense of Obamacare. It seems that even four election cycles (and the loss of more than 1,000 seats in local, state, and federal legislatures) of voter retribution has failed to dampen progressive enthusiasm for President Barack Obama's signature health care reform. This devotion to Obamacare is in one sense not surprising, since the law represents a tangible first step toward their ultimate goal: single-payer, government-sponsored health care.

At times, a sampling of Democrats will admit to Obamacare's deficiencies, but usually in the context of condemning cold-blooded Republicans who turned the taxpayer faucet off just when Obamacare's subsidies were most needed. (Note that this narrative ignores the ugly irony that the intended beneficiaries of additional taxpayer largesse are the big, bad insurance carriers who require subsidies in order to keep offering plans that are otherwise unprofitable.)

It is now eight years later, and decision time draws near. A "replace" bill will have profound consequences for our health care delivery system. Accordingly, this is the time and place when real political leaders earn their money—and their legacies.

The left smells a paper tiger. They know many Republicans like to talk the talk at Lincoln Day dinners, that throwing spitballs from the bleachers is the easiest thing to do in politics.

But it's a different ballgame when real votes bring real consequences to real people. Suddenly, your "safe seat" is competitive because the Democrats have run a million dollars of "mediscare" commercials against you.

The bottom line: Democrats do not believe enough Republicans have the chutzpah to make tough votes, that the GOP lacks the courage to eliminate goodies previously awarded to the voters—especially when a government entitlement program is at issue.

Something close to the Senate health care draft can counter this narrative, especially one that includes the modernization that transitions Medicaid to per capita block grants and returns all enrollees to the traditional (approximately) 50/50 federal/state match rate that existed prior to Obamacare. Recall many governors of both parties bought into Obamacare in order to access Washington's "free money" for new able-bodied enrollees, a win-win for fans of the welfare state, and a "success" that has resulted in one in four Americans now covered by the program.

But their "victory" has helped further expose Medicaid's subpar service regime. The number of participating physicians has dropped as reimbursements are cut, while Medicaid spending continues to exert immense pressure on federal and state budget deficits. Indeed, Medicaid spending now represents 10 percent of the entire federal budget.

The Senate draft is therefore a rare opportunity to control what amounts to an open-ended federal entitlement. This is a big deal.

A decent compromise on Obamacare's community rating mandate is another step in the right direction. As discussed in previous columns, expanded pricing options as a function of age more accurately reflect market costs even with the inclusion of pre-existing disclaimers.

A potentially winning Republican narrative emerges: Able-bodied, non-poor men are given the opportunity and (responsibility) to purchase an insurance policy that best suits their circumstances. The vast majority of this healthy subgroup will be covered by inexpensive, high-deductible catastrophic policies while people who have experienced more problematic health histories (those with pre-existing conditions) will continue to have access to affordable health coverage.

Note the Senate draft does not contain the House repeal of Obamacare's taxes—presumably to mute the Democrats' mantra of "tax cuts for the rich and service cuts to the poor." This will of course not diminish Democratic fondness for class warfare rhetoric, but it does free up dollars to meet GOP moderates' demands for additional spending on out-of-pocket costs and the opioid epidemic (albeit not enough to date).

The endgame is fully in the GOP's court. Few of its supporters will be satisfied with a failed attempt at "repeal and wait for two years." Rather, the choice is clear: Either lead or be exposed, either wilt or show the voters that a federal entitlement can be reformed, either pass a bill that lowers premiums or expect a "what for?" from voters come November 2018.

How wonderful it would be if the GOP chose to compete—pass a bill, celebrate health care choice—and then went out and won the 2018 midterms on a "can do" platform.

One can dream, right?

CHAPTER 5

Calamity Central: How To Fix Urban America

Politics can be complicated. A case in point is the federal government's long-running War on Poverty. President Lyndon Baines Johnson's brainchild is now more than fifty years old. Various estimates peg its price tag in the neighborhood of $23 trillion. It has spawned hundreds of satellite programs (and tens of thousands of bureaucrats) under the direction of both political parties. And by any measure, it has (and we have) lost the war.

My purpose is not to recite annual poverty rates or various measures of accompanying dysfunction such as underperforming public schools, fatherlessness, homelessness, substance abuse, gun violence, joblessness, or incarceration rates. These familiar realities of urban life are well documented; their devastating impact can be observed from the window of any Amtrak train traveling north between Baltimore, Maryland, and New York City.

Rather, America's mission going forward must be to see things as they are, not as we wish them to be. But a willingness to engage the former requires an open mind—a difficult exercise, as the defenders of the indefensible reflexively invoke victimology to explain continuing welfare state dysfunction. These good folks never run out of pejoratives ("racism," "sexism," "capitalism," or some other "-ism") to explain why expensive government programs so often fail.

We who live in the real world must reject this formula. Public-sector programs have underperformed for far too long. Too much money has been wasted. Too many opportunities have been missed. Too many young lives have been lost or cut short. Some might think that decades of obvious failure would spur people of goodwill to action. Sometimes it does, but not nearly enough. Too often, it is the activists who claim to care the most that prove to be the strongest defenders of a dysfunctional status quo. Why?

A lifetime in politics provides insight. Chronic situations result from lack of vision—an inability to reach beyond the "comfort zone" better known as the status quo. This deadly condition has conspired to wreak havoc within our urban areas for more than half a century.

For progressives, the answer is *always* more dollars—ever more dollars to fix an endless list of social ills. These dollars fund a firmly ingrained poverty infrastructure that does not plan to go quietly into the night. But the Trump era gives pause. The president and a GOP Congress means increased accountability rather than an endless supply of no-questions-asked greenbacks. Such quantification also brings repercussions for failure. This is how Donald Trump runs his world. It's a workplace discipline borrowed from business—a space that requires measurement.

Conventional wisdom says the private-sector formula will not work in Washington, DC—that even Ronald Reagan could not constrain the poverty bureaucracy. As if to confirm the notion, the beginning of the Trump era witnessed a familiar resistance. Early media reports described active opposition on the part of selected bureaucrats—maybe not such a good idea with this new sheriff. Mr. Trump will take names—he is even known to fire people—but can he make a difference?

Read on to learn more about the initial skirmishes of what will be years of a monumental battle of wills.

On Baltimore

May 28, 2015, *Weekly Standard*

One unexplained death. So many negative images. So many pundits talking past real issues. So many obvious problems.

The storylines of Baltimore's latest riots are heavy fodder for observers from all sides of the political spectrum.

On the left, it's mostly about racism and bad cops and not enough social spending. The Ferguson-inspired slogan "Black Lives Matter" is renewed even though in the spate of highly publicized recent young black deaths there is no evidence that Michael Brown, who attacked a police officer, was deprived of any rights at all.

In Baltimore, the mayor turns to the feds in order to investigate her allegedly out-of-control police. A newly elected state's attorney promises to answer the angry mob's cries for justice. Yet, nobody asks the (indelicate) question of why the mayor and her chief prosecutor waited for Freddie Gray's death before asking for federal intervention. Another indelicate question: Where was the street rage when one-sixth of the population of Baltimore was arrested in 2005?

On the right, it's a more complex debate, including the facts and circumstances of Mr. Gray's arrest and transport that fateful morning. Besides police process and procedure, I and so many others bemoan the considerable social ills that poison West Baltimore neighborhoods: too many pregnant teenagers, too many sick babies, too many fatherless children, too many single-income households, too many high school dropouts, too many welfare dependents, too few manufacturing jobs, too much drug culture, too little hope.

Our conclusion is familiar: Trillions of dollars directed into poor communities over the past fifty years has failed to produce better neighborhoods. Just too many left behind, with little hope. It seems a valueless culture trumps social welfare programs every time.

Going forward, it's not nearly good enough to ritualistically repeat the usual clichés regarding the importance of "healing" and "coming together." Here, we truly need to define our terms.

Healing is not about demanding your unique definition of justice or threatening to burn the place down if your demands are not met. Neither is it about a not-so-secret war on African Americans in a police department where the mayor, police commissioner, and nearly 50 percent of the force is black. Real healing is respecting the criminal justice system's search for truth and then working within the system for change if you disagree with the result. Kind of like Dr. King taught us to think and act.

Similarly, coming together is great if it means everybody working to bring about positive change—in this case, bringing the police closer to the community they are paid to protect and rooting out bad actors within the department along the way. There may be bad cops, but the Baltimore riots were not explained by a reaction to bad police work.

Most important, progress will only come if we are willing to think *really big and long-term*. Such a new way of thinking about our inner cities would include parental demands for better schools, community leaders lobbying businesses to reinvest in their neighborhoods, political leaders willing to alleviate the dis-incentivizing impacts of high property taxes, a recognition that teenage pregnancy is a key predictor of cultural dysfunction, and a willingness to admit that young boys desperately need a strong male influence in their lives.

Leaders from both sides of the aisle will be willing to go "all in" if our leaders can shake off their Great Society blinders. Yes, big-time barriers will always be present—not the least of which is a newfound challenge to widespread acceptance of social welfarism, a central tenet of today's progressive thought. But the case against government subsidy and dependence grows day by day, month by month, year by year.

On the other side, the right must pursue reform of criminal sentencing laws and seek to better understand the rage—frustration—bitterness—that flashed across America's television screens two weeks ago. Such a task is far easier said than done as most conservatives live a life far removed from the realities of inner city life.

The bottom line: The issue in Baltimore is poverty far more than race. (After all, Baltimore has been a one-party town controlled by African Americans for decades.) People who grow up in stable families, attend functional schools, and are surrounded with examples of economic mobility simply do not riot when something goes wrong in their community.

Short-term solutions yield short-term peace.

Time to pray—and get to work.

Giuliani's New York, Shattered

August 27, 2015, *Weekly Standard*

As New York suffers through yet another challenging era of ineffective political leadership, it is worthwhile to recall what one leader can accomplish under the most difficult circumstances.

Context here is New York, New York, circa the bad old days of the 1980s. Many of that era's pundits had decided to write off the Big Apple. The David Dinkins era was the nadir—rampant crime, dangerous schools, a declining real estate market, and a depressed (and fleeing) small business community—a scene reminiscent of the bleeding, burning New York of the 1960s.

Then there came along a tough-talking, crime-fighting former federal prosecutor with a can-do attitude and willingness to mix it up with the most strident progressives of the time. His name was Rudy Giuliani—and he was a Republican in a town where Democrats enjoyed an overwhelming registration advantage.

But he knew how to lead. Specifically, he understood the need to identify what was broken and then fix it in a quantifiable way. And so the Giuliani administration instituted a "broken windows" crime-fighting strategy whereby law enforcement was empowered to draw a line in the sand at the commission of minor offenses. In the process, a newfound sense of security was delivered to a worn-down populous more than fed up with the great city's obvious decline.

New York's monumental turnaround has been well documented by observers right and left. As they say, statistics don't lie, and in the case of Giuliani's New York, the statistics were dramatic. How dramatic? A $2 billion deficit turned into a multibillion-dollar surplus, a 58 percent decline in welfare rolls, a 56 percent decrease in violent crime between 1993 to 2001 (the number of street cops increased from 28,000 to 40,000), a public-private partnership cleaned up Times Square, high performing charter schools exploded, small businesses returned, and tourism made dramatic gains. The Big Apple was back.

Of course, many people contributed along the way, not the least of which was a police force newly reengaged in restoring a great city's pride. But it was the unrelenting drive of one indispensable man that turned it around.

History records that a "Giuliani-Light" administration followed under the leadership of Michael Bloomberg: "Giuliani" because many of Rudy's crime and economic policies were kept in place, "Light" because the billionaire-turned-politician also displayed an un-Giuliani-like proclivity for government interference into individual liberty—the popularity of Big Gulps and sugary desserts notwithstanding.

Fast-forward to Gotham 2015 and the delusory administration of Mayor Bill de Blasio. You have to give it to the new anti-Giuliani—he never sought to hide the uber-progressivism of his program. Indeed, year one of the de Blasio administration has borne witness to the worst inclinations of the progressive agenda.

The only problem is that progressivism *does not work* outside of certain college campuses and Washington, DC. In the real world of markets and wealth mobility, calls for massive tax increases (a proposed "mansion tax") have started another exodus of the wealthy. (If you recall the great State of Maryland losing one-third of its millionaires in the year after passage of Martin O'Malley's millionaire's tax in 2009, please go to the head of the class.)

But the damage is not confined to the economic realm. The attempted redirection of funds intended for the city's spectacularly successful charter schools was fully in line with the teachers' union agenda. Sanctuary city status prohibits the police from inquiring into legal status *and* guarantees access to taxpayer-financed welfare benefits. And de Blasio's deeply grounded disregard for law enforcement was again on prominent display in the days and weeks following Ferguson and its progeny (yet not without remarkable displays of anti-de Blasio sentiment from the rank and file in the aftermath of the cold-blooded murders of two of New York's finest).

If you thought that de Blasio would take a break after the unrelenting negative coverage of his police problems...think again. Only within the past few weeks did a federal judge save NYC's banks from catastrophe by finding the city's attempt to impose "socially responsible" lending practices on them unconstitutional. For those of you who lived through our recent mortgage crisis and recession, this attempted shakedown of local banks to benefit progressive causes brings back bad memories of ACORN and its activist progeny. The former community organizer in the White House was no doubt disappointed.

Your local bookstore is chock-full of "how-to" leadership manuals. Indeed, how to prod massive bureaucracies to work more efficiently is always going to be a hot topic in think-tank world. Most of these books analyze the power of one individual to effectuate change. But citizens beware: This well-detailed power cuts *both ways* when voters screw it up.

The "city that never sleeps" is again in steady, serious decline.

Our old friend "Frankie" would not be happy.

Neither should you.

Guest Commentary: Sharpen Focus on Best Ways to Win the War on Poverty

January 20, 2016, *Naples Daily News*
Note: This post was coauthored by Vann Ellison.

Deep-rooted challenges facing our country often simmer in the background during election years because they have been with us for generations, failing to garner headlines or "trend" on Twitter feeds.

Or they may receive only token acknowledgement among national priorities in the case of President Obama's final State of the Union address last week. One such challenge is President Lyndon Johnson's War on Poverty, which created the modern welfare state and the mixed results in achieving its mission a half-century later.

With all the arguments about income inequality, one would think helping those struggling to get on the bottom rungs of the economic ladder would be front and center on the national agenda. After all, there has been constant talk over the last several years about the "unfairness" of compensation for corporate CEOs, hedge fund managers, and whoever else is deemed to be in the top 1 percent of economic achievement.

Another way to address income inequality is to modernize an outdated system to better help the bottom 15 percent, or 46 million Americans, escape poverty.

Fortunately, a policy forum held in the key primary state of South Carolina this month did just that. Including several presidential candidates, the event raised concerns about how effective this so-called war, waged largely from government office buildings in Washington, DC, has been.

Named after legendary public servant Jack Kemp, the forum recalled his legacy of expanding economic opportunity for all. Whether the subject of intense media scrutiny on the mean streets of Baltimore or largely hidden from public view in relatively wealthy Naples, poverty remains America's No. 1 social ill.

House Speaker Paul Ryan, one of the co-moderators and a protégé of Kemp, defined the problem of the "poverty trap" caused by a tax code and welfare system that rewards benefits and penalizes work. Equally important, he described how the last fifty years have witnessed the advent of eighty unique, non-coordinated anti-poverty programs targeted to every need imaginable. The bottom line: The nation's poverty rate is nearly 15 percent, having changed little since the 1960s.

Each year, the Government Accountability Office (the watchdog auditing function of Congress) documents fragmentation, duplication, and overlap among the nation's annual $1 trillion worth of poverty assistance programs, which they maintain adversely impacts service delivery. What this means in practice is at any given time the wrong benefits are provided to the wrong people—hardly the type of targeted relief required. Moreover, soon after, Congress forgets what they have authorized; programs are put on bureaucratic autopilot.

Anyone interested in achieving results with the federal government, whether as a governor attempting to effectively implement programs statewide or the head of a nonprofit trying to make them work on the streets, has experienced the utter frustration of applying for federal waivers or having to follow program "guidance."

Such terms are Washington-speak for bureaucratic procedure, which is what happens when "inputs" are measured instead of "outputs." Government does a fine job of measuring resources going into programs but is far less concerned about how many individuals secure employment.

Florida's presidential candidates are among those who understand the need to empower individuals, not government.

Senator Marco Rubio highlighted his flex grant plan, which would allow state and local entities more power to innovate and develop initiatives that meet local priorities. Championing the free enterprise system, he undercut arguments from the political left about income inequality, saying it's the only system in the world that can make poor people richer without making rich people poorer.

Former Governor Jeb Bush, who released a plan to devolve funding to the states, talked about how compassion should never be measured in dollars, only results.

Governor John Kasich is coordinating the myriad government assistance programs in Ohio and advancing the concept of states being the "laboratories of democracy" through innovation. For example, combining employment opportunities and welfare assistance into one facility would end the practice of rubber-stamping people through the system without addressing the need for a job.

The well-respected community activist Bob Woodson condemned both political parties, accusing Republicans of insufficient sensitivity to the underclass, while Democrats continue their victimization rhetoric.

Despite the absence of Democratic presidential candidates at the forum, we may yet see the two parties describe their respective solutions for expanding opportunity and eliminating poverty before this election is over. That would not only capture the public's attention, but it would renew a second "War on Poverty."

This is the war Kemp started and the one we should finish as a matter of common decency.

Bob Ehrlich on What Ails Baltimore, One Year Later

May 19, 2016, *MarylandReporter.com*
Note: This post was coauthored by Jim Pettit.

Over a year has passed since Baltimore erupted in violent protests following the death of Freddie Gray and, predictably, the respective political parties propose vastly different remedies for what ails "Charm City."

Progressives (those political actors formerly known as "liberals") seek to double down on the status quo. These folks focus on the need for increased social spending—and ever more government. On the other side of the aisle, many conservatives view the plight of Freddie Gray as one of welfare state (and, possibly, law enforcement) failure.

Without doubt, America's leading progressives believe expansive government is the answer. Democratic front-runner Hillary Clinton, in a recent Maryland campaign stop, promised to direct "hundreds of billions" of dollars in new investments in urban America. President Obama, in a post-riot press conference last year, complained that desperately needed "mass investments" for inner city revival would never materialize in a Republican Congress. Senator Bernie Sanders, for his part, labeled Mr. Gray's neighborhood a "third-world country" a few months ago. (How ironic that Mr. Sanders' voting record helped make it so).

Always Calling for More "Investment"

The common denominator for this crowd is more "investment"; always more "investment"; never enough "investment." Note that the left co-opted this capitalist term some time ago. It implies that every taxpayer dime spent in Baltimore and elsewhere magically yields a measurable return. A case in point is the proposed Baltimore $3 billion subway line Governor Larry Hogan terminated last summer over cost concerns. In a recent Baltimore campaign stop, local transportation expert Clinton took issue with the decision—to widespread acclaim. Not surprisingly, Ms. Clinton's mass transit plan is all about spending money where the votes are—not so much for where the efficiencies lie.

Recall that it has long been standard practice for Maryland politicians to steer local aid to Baltimore City. The vast majority of this money goes to public schools, where over $900 million, or approximately $15,000 per student, is now spent. This per student amount is almost always the highest among Maryland's twenty-four subdivisions.

Education Spending Hasn't Produced Results

Unfortunately, this money pit continues to reward failure. Baltimore City's public schools produce the lowest SAT scores of any Maryland subdivision. More students drop out of high school here than anywhere else statewide. And the public school system hires the least number of "highly qualified teachers." It has been a perennial fight to get air conditioners installed in classrooms. And students at nearly one hundred city schools continue to use bottled water almost ten years after lead was discovered in their drinking fountains.

Such dysfunction is by now familiar to all of us. But not to worry, the federal government has come to the rescue—with a grant. The U.S. Department of Education will now fund social workers and psychologists to provide therapy sessions to students believed to be traumatized by last year's riots. This new program will allegedly help our students recover from "a violent event in which the learning environment has been disrupted." If only periodic street unrest was the dominant cause of so much educational failure!

The plight of our public schools is only one of many problems plaguing Baltimore. The dysfunctions are familiar—and ever present: too many pregnant teenagers, too many sick babies, too many fatherless children, too many single-income households, too many high school dropouts, too many welfare dependents, too few manufacturing jobs, too much drug culture, too much gang violence, too little hope. Government failures encourage these trends at worst; at best, hyper-expensive government solutions do little to fix them.

Legacy of Mass Arrests

One issue unique in Baltimore's recent history is its legacy of mass arrests—that horrific political policy foisted on the police and the African American citizens of Baltimore ten years ago. Recall this was not DWB ("Driving While Black"). Rather, it was BWB ("Breathing While Black"). Thousands of innocent people rounded up and placed in custody—and all to get those all-important public safety stats looking healthier for campaign consumption. Sadly, said policy resulted in approximately one-sixth of the population of Baltimore placed under arrest—in one year! The legacy of such negligence rings clear: For young men like Freddie Gray, career choices often mean whether or not to flee from the police.

No discussion about Baltimore is complete without citing its self-inflicted tax burden. Consider that its property and income taxes are the highest statewide. Added to this is an onerous capital equipment levy on business—twice that of other Maryland subdivisions that impose the tax. The predictable result: Baltimore is America's largest city without a Fortune 500 company.

A radically different approach to a city on the brink is desperately needed. Anything less and the "post–Freddie Gray era" will look remarkably similar to the status quo—an unacceptable proposition for those of us who grew up in and around this once great American city.

A Radical Solution to End Poverty

February 16, 2017, *Baltimore Business Journal*

Federal involvement in anti-poverty programs has roots in the 1930s' New Deal. Job training and housing assistance were early priorities for Franklin Delano Roosevelt's policy gurus. Three decades later, creating rental vouchers and public housing developments became a major focus of Lyndon Baines Johnson's "War on Poverty."

I could fill volumes with the good intentions and inevitable controversies attendant to such vision. But good intentions do not a stable neighborhood make. Suffice it to say that the best of plans often go awry when the federal government mandates a one-size-fits-all, throw-money-at-the-problem approach.

But it is no longer good enough to rely on "best intentions." America has left too many marginalized people behind for far too long.

The numbers speak for themselves:

In 2015, there were 43 million people in poverty and 19.4 million in "deep poverty" (households with a total income below 50 percent of the federal poverty threshold).

On a single night in 2016, 550,000 people experienced homelessness in the U.S., including nearly 40,000 veterans and 77,500 individuals experiencing chronic homelessness.

More than one in five children in America is poor and nearly four out of ten families with single mothers live in poverty.

Nearly 9 percent of all children live in deep poverty.

These and similar startling statistics will become familiar to the general public as the media refocuses on issues of poverty and homelessness under a Republican administration. This favored tactic of left-leaning pundits should not dissuade the Trump administration from instituting a new approach to homelessness and its associated maladies, however.

Indeed, an energized Trump coalition distrustful of uber-expensive federal programs is eager to investigate outside-the-box remedies to America's most intractable problems. And why not start at a place where a dramatically new program is enjoying real success?

Meet the not-for-profit St. Matthew's House located in Naples, Florida. CEO Vann Ellison has run the operation since 2004 with no government subsidy; potential clients are asked to make at least some sliding-scale payment in exchange for St. Matthew's House services.

Ellison says his mission is to provide individuals with the requisite skills to defeat a dependence culture—one that is supported by $744 billion in annual federal spending on eighty separate programs covering every human need imaginable. Conversely, Ellison's program is a private-sector success orientated with job training and employment obtained through St. Matthew's catering, thrift store, and car wash businesses. Ellison is not interested in simply taking low-hanging fruit, either. Florida's opiate epidemic led Ellison to add a year-long, spiritually inspired program that boasts a 97 percent success rate as measured by individuals staying sober for at least twelve months.

Campaign 2016 saw Donald Trump famously ask urban America to give him a look because he "could not do worse." For this he was ostracized by the defenders of the poverty establishment.

But here in southwest Florida is the perfect model for the Trump era. Here, tucked away on the economically deprived side of an otherwise prosperous town, is a successful, faith-based, long-term, entrepreneur-inspired operation willing to measure itself and report its findings to the community at large.

Many of our largest urban areas continue to suffer from the specter of multigenerational poverty despite housing and homelessness programs that have eaten up trillions of taxpayer dollars since the Johnson administration.

One takeaway is that secular government-sponsored welfare programs always underperform. We expect too much of them. They do

not change hearts or transform lives. It is not how they are designed...
and so why not try something different—something radical—something made of equal parts independence and self-reliance? We could not do worse.

CHAPTER 6

A New World Order

Campaign 2016 presented the seventeen Republican candidates for president with an unexpected force of nature: Donald J. Trump. This candidate would *not* follow traditional rules of engagement. Fundraising was placed on the back burner. "White papers" would not be his cup of tea. And indictments directed at his fellow competitors—often made in rapid-fire succession—would be intensely personal. This novel approach generated numerous awkward give-and-takes during debate season, but none uglier than a Trump suggestion that President George W. Bush *knew* Saddam Hussein did not possess weapons of mass destruction at the time he ordered the invasion of Iraq. A separate Trump assertion that "43" was partly to blame for 9/11 was equally disdainful—but somehow less newsworthy.

Such accusations were manna from heaven for Bush haters everywhere, as it bolstered the Democrats' oft-repeated refrain: "Bush lied, people died." For conservatives, the charge cut to the heart of the Bush legacy and was accordingly viewed as disqualifying by establishment Republicans. Vice President Cheney and Governor Jeb Bush (among others) shot back at Trump in the strongest terms. Neo-cons and conservative periodicals such as *National Review* and *The Weekly Standard* jumped on the bandwagon. Nevertheless, the Trump train rolled on with relatively little resulting damage. Here, "us versus them" played to Trump's anti-establishment narrative.

Pundits marveled at Trump's survival skills, but the comment flushed out something far more pertinent—many rank-and-file Republicans had come to view the Iraqi war as a Bush-era foreign policy blunder regardless of whether the president had a good faith conviction about Saddam's alleged WMDs.

This highly charged remark provided insight into Trump's worldview. *His* administration would not be cavalier in sacrificing U.S. blood and treasure in foreign entanglements—the campaign to eliminate ISIS notwithstanding. This was Trump's iteration of "America First" (in reality a pre-World War II isolationist rally cry), and in his view far less about UN and NATO initiatives and far more about a bolstered U.S. military able to make the world's most notorious troublemakers (Iran, China, North Korea, and Russia) think twice about repeating their Obama-era provocations. Cruise missiles in Syria and really big bombs in Afghanistan would supply early context for those media types who confused "America First" with American retreat. Further refinement would occur on the world stage at the UN wherein the new American president would jettison diplomatic protocol in order to call out the world's most notorious problem children, especially North Korea's Kim Jong-un, aka "Rocket Man." Here, the new president revisited the proposition that our enemies should fear U.S. might—and that such a mindset would make the world a safer place. After all, the "crazy, warmongering" indictment was also made against the robustly demonized Ronald Reagan. Seems that one turned out pretty good.

Still, Trump's early foreign policy pronouncements were easily distinguished from Reagan in at least one baseline respect: Russia. In a weird twist, Democrats found themselves on the hawkish end of the policy paradigm. Talk about killing two birds with one stone: Progressives could degrade Trump's win by citing Russian hacking attempts against the DNC and Clinton campaign and question why a Republican president (of all people) would seek to indulge the murderous former KGB agent in the Kremlin, all the while ignoring Obama's infamous disparaging of then–presidential candidate Romney's warning about the dangers of Russia in their 2012 debate.

The media adopted the new narrative with glee. First, National Security Director Mike Flynn was forced to resign for failing to inform Vice President Pence about pre-inaugural conversations with Russian officials. Then Attorney General Jeff Sessions recused himself from his department's Russian influence investigation when it was revealed he too had failed to recall a meeting with the Russian ambassador while he was acting in his capacity as a sitting U.S. Senator. Finally, FBI Director James Comey made yet another appearance on the national stage (his last one as Director it turns out) to assure all concerned that his agency was indeed investigating any inappropriate contacts between Russian operatives and the Trump campaign.

Each event fed the "Russian hacking" storyline. The progressive cable networks gave regular coverage to the "scandal." What better nullification storyline could Trump haters attach themselves to than this one? In response, leading Democrats repeatedly requested an independent prosecutor, a demand subsequently granted by Deputy Attorney General Rod Rosenstein in the person of former FBI Director Robert Mueller. Yet the high-profile memory failures and what-if scenarios could not sustain the narrative forever—no evidence was produced to show how Russian-sponsored hacking had impacted the election results. Nevertheless, many high-profile Republicans experienced difficulty coming up with a rational explanation for the new president's benign characterizations of the former KGB agent intent on reconstituting the Russian Empire.

How Obama Made Sure to Leave Every Part of the World More Dangerous than He Found It

May 11, 2015, *National Review*

> *I will meet with not just our allies and our friends, but I will initiate tough diplomacy with our enemies. That includes Syria, Iran, North Korea, and Venezuela. I would meet with them, and I would meet with them without preconditions.*
>
> —Barack Obama, May 16, 2008

> *On all of these issues, but particularly missile defense, this can be solved, but it is important for [Putin] to give me space.... This is my last election. After my election I have more flexibility.*
>
> —President Obama to former Russian president Medvedev, March 26, 2012

The former promise was uttered during Senator Obama's initial run for the presidency. It was intended for consumption by his anti-war base and to let the world know the zero-sum worldview of the Reagan-Bush era was (finally) extinguished. The latter was not intended for public consumption but was nevertheless captured by omnipresent audio during an unguarded moment between the two principals. Both statements genuinely reflect the baseline foreign-policy values and reflexive passivity of our forty-fourth president. You see, Barack Obama was always secure in the belief that the constant projection of American military power was the primary reason for anti-American sentiment around the world.

Alas, seven years later, a seemingly endless stream of apologies, attempts to placate the world's miscreants, and inappropriate stabs at moral equivalency are primary components of a spectacularly failed U.S. foreign policy. Seems the "cowboy" Bush and all those opportunistic militarists at the Pentagon are not the reason so many bad guys take issue with the U.S. Similarly, the infamous time-dishonored plea for time regarding negotiations with Russia speaks to a comfortable familiarity with weak negotiating positions. With regard to Putin, "flexibility" can be read as "I have to look tough now, but just wait until I'm safely elected to a second term—then I'll feel free to cut a deal—any deal."

This "anything goes" desire to cut deals and refrain from antagonizing bad guys (and, in the process, finally earning that Nobel Peace Prize so gratuitously awarded in 2009) explains a problematic series of policy decisions that has worried our allies and allowed our enemies daily batting practice at U.S. expense.

To wit:

- An early world apology tour, focused on the Muslim world, during which the newly elected U.S. president issued mea culpas for alleged inappropriate U.S. actions around the world; interestingly, no mention was made or concern evidenced of considerable U.S. blood spent to save Muslim lives.

- The expedient selling out of Poland and the Czech Republic on missile defense in the interest of an oversold "reset" with Putin's Russia.

- A quick and forceful condemnation of Egyptian president Hosni Mubarak in the aftermath of his country's "Arab Spring" street protests—to the benefit of the viscerally anti-democratic, ruthless, and anti-American Muslim Brotherhood.

- A missed opportunity to gain negotiating leverage with a weakened Iranian regime by failing to support the dissident Green Movement in Iran, circa 2009.

- A historic breach (complete with personal insults) with a sitting Israeli prime minister who has the fortitude to place Israel's security interest ahead of Mr. Obama's nuclear legacy.

- An infamous "line in the sand" when proof of Syrian dictator Bashar Assad's use of weapons of mass destruction against Syrian rebels was revealed to the world, but forgotten when the U.S. began relying on Iranian boots on the ground to fight the formerly J.V. army known as ISIS.

- The trade of five varsity terrorists taken from Guantanamo Bay (of whom at least three are suspected to have returned to the battlefield) for the AWOL sergeant Bowe Bergdahl.

- An opening to diplomatic relations with the repressive Raúl Castro without securing the release and/or extradition of political prisoners and wanted U.S. fugitives.

- A framework "agreement" announcement on the Iranian nuclear deal, followed in short order by harsh condemnation by Ayatollah Khamenei and a host of unanswered issues, including schedule(s) for sanctions relief, a process for sanctions relief, conditions attached to periodic inspections, a schedule for unfreezing Iranian assets, and a framework for dispute resolution. The bottom line: The president has never been a comfortable commander-in-chief when placing American lives and military assets in harm's way; yet, the reflexive peace candidate seems ever ready, willing, and able to negotiate with the world's most notorious bad guys—always from a position of weakness, always leaving the world just a bit more insecure than he found it. When it comes to so-called "peace" negotiations with the world's tyrants, it seems America is always open for (condition-less) business, a legacy that has and will continue to make Americans—and the free world—less safe.

A Vote for Trump Is a Vote Against Softness

July 7, 2016, *Washington Examiner*

President Theodore Roosevelt famously admonished America to "speak softly, and carry a big stick." Yet, today, a progressive president incubated in the anti-war movement is successfully doubling down on the former and all but eviscerating the latter. And soft power is not the only weak aspect of Obama's transformed America.

The trends are difficult to ignore:

- Identity politics is now taught to young people in a way that our most liberal friends would have rejected not so long ago.

However antithetical to American individualism it may be to believe that one's sex, race, or ethnicity must be determinative in one's politics, it has nevertheless garnered the endorsement of the progressive movement. For context, note the relentless hostility directed toward conservative African Americans from leaders of the civil rights industry—at no cost to the purveyors. A more ludicrous example is Madeleine Albright's feminist indictment that "there is a special place in hell for women who don't help each other," i.e., provide conditionless support for Hillary Clinton's presidential campaign. Yes, you read that correctly: One's reproductive organs must dictate one's political identity—at least according to our former Secretary of State.

- Nowhere is the soft label more appropriate than on our college and university campuses.

Today, speech codes complete with safe zones, trigger warnings, and microaggressions are as much a part of the collegiate experience as history, math, and literature.

Indeed, what were unthinkable limitations on academic free speech a mere ten years ago are now widely accepted notions at many of our leading institutions of higher learning.

Think about how devalued speech has become: The great-grand-children of the "greatest generation" are now told they have a right to an offense-less life and to run (not walk) to the nearest safe zone should unpleasant language or events (presumably from the College Republicans or Fox News) impinge on them in a negative way. The widespread acceptance of such practices can also be attributed to poor parenting; how else to explain why such coddled young adults could be so easily influenced?

All of which begs the question of how long it will take for some enterprising union rep to negotiate the imposition(s) of safe zones into the private-sector workplace?

- The anti-war candidate won (twice) and (sort of) exited American might stage left.

Unfortunately, military withdrawals from Afghanistan and Iraq were accomplished with little regard for the smoldering vacuums left behind. Today, such smoldering embers have morphed into a full-scale fire. President Obama also led a world apology tour wherein the "mea culpas" were freely offered for Uncle Sam's imperialism and intemperate behavior regarding the Muslim world. But history intervened. You see, miscreants migrate toward vacuums. Bad guys smell "safe." Autocratic bullies are always happy to exploit the weak.

No pundit could seriously feign surprise when the former community organizer adopted an unserious approach to the Islamic State, aka "the J.V. squad," or that he happily supplied the enemy with the precise timetable for U.S. withdrawal on the few occasions he agreed to deploy troops. But leave it to a former anti-war Senator to define soft in the context of modern warfare; who could forget John Kerry's pitiful announcement that a U.S. bombing campaign in Syria promised to be a "very limited, very targeted, very short-term effort...[an] unbelievably small, limited kind of effort"? Bashar Assad no doubt shook in his boots upon reading that missive from a U.S. administration always uncomfortable with the projection of U.S. military assets around the world.

Yet, such rhetoric goes hand in hand with insufficiently narrow rules of engagement that have contributed to the increasingly strong suspicion among our Sunni allies that the U.S. is not in the terror war to win—too soft, so to speak.

The administration's approach is nowhere better exemplified than by the decision to send '70s anti-war crooner James Taylor to Paris (rather than travel to massive unity rallies attended by other world leaders) in the aftermath of the Charlie Hebdo terror attack. Now, "You've Got a Friend" is one of my favorite tunes, but don't you think the message would have been a wee bit stronger had the leader of the free world bothered to show up to deliver it?

- Back home, the war against football plays here too, as Obama has stated that if he had sons they would not be encouraged to play America's most popular sport.

But here, at least, the soft card may be unsuccessful. Football appeals to the American sense of competitiveness—you know—that personality trait that makes you want to keep score. Some commentators even believe this uniquely American game plays a part in our "exceptionalism." Oops, forgot—Obama's definition of American exceptionalism has proven to be far different from what so many of us (still) believe makes Uncle Sam so unique: individualism, assimilation, laissez-faire capitalism, work ethic, upward mobility.

If you believe cultural "softness" is metastasizing throughout our culture, consider voting for Donald Trump. He does not have all the answers, but I'll take "great" over "soft" every time.

Obama's Foreign Policy: Much Given, Little Gained

September 2, 2016, *Washington Examiner*

As the final days of the Obama administration approach, it's appropriate to review the record. WARNING: NOT FOR THE FAINT OF HEART!

Russia

Remember when the newly elected president and his Secretary of State declared a "reset" with Vladimir Putin? Who better to make America forget the cowboy Bush than a man who was literally raised to be a progressive, anti-war activist? And while "W" said he could see a partner in peace in good ole Vlad, this president was determined to simply placate the Russian president in hopes of making peace with the newly ascendant bear.

Such indulgence has not worked. Today Russia runs amok in Ukraine and across much of the Middle East through its proxies in Syria, Iraq, Lebanon, Sudan, and Iran. U.S. allies have taken notice: America's consistently passive response to Putin's aggression has encouraged Egypt, Jordan, Saudi Arabia, and the UAE to question American resolve throughout the troubled region—especially with regard to Iran.

Last week, media reports surfaced of increased Russian troop deployments to the Ukrainian border. No "reset" dividends for the good guys....

Cuba

In March, a triumphant Barack Obama arrived in Havana "to bury the last remnant of the Cold War." Fifty years of Cold War antagonism notwithstanding, this American president was determined to ignore the voices of Cuban dissidents—and open the island nation to all sorts of travel, trade, and hard currency goodies from their American friends.

But no sooner had Obama left than those persistent Castros returned to their old hobbies of arresting, torturing, and beating up pro-democracy dissidents. State repression has only worsened since Obama's alleged new era of cooperation. Seems Mr. Obama forgot to remind Raúl Castro that "normalization" was supposed to lead to the restoration of the most basic of human rights. Oh well, the Cuban gulag might still be operational, but you can bet all sorts of folks can't wait for those shiny new casinos to reopen on Havana Beach....

Iran

After-the-fact confessions from the likes of Obama alter ego Ben Rhodes confirm what many observers suspected all along: Mr. Obama was intent on striking a nuclear deal with the Iranian mullahs seemingly regardless of consequences.

As a result, Iran enjoys renewed international legitimacy, an intact military infrastructure, and $180 billion in sanctions relief. The U.S. has been rewarded with nothing but increased harassment of U.S. Navy ships in the Strait of Hormuz and renewed scorn from the Iranian propaganda machine.

Today, Iran doubles down on anti-American, anti-Israel rhetoric while Mr. Obama "settles" a $400 million, forty-seven-year-old "debt" (in cold cash) at precisely the same time five American hostages are set free. All just a fortuitous set of circumstances, assures the Obama State Department.

Want to wager how many additional concessions Ayatollah Khomeini can exact from a legacy-preoccupied Mr. Obama over the next four months?

Guantanamo Bay

The president and his progressive acolytes regularly proclaim that the U.S. detention facility at Guantanamo Bay is a useful recruiting tool for terrorists the world over. Hence, his campaign promise to close the military prison.

But it has proven exceedingly difficult to find other "homes" for the worst of the worst terror soldiers. Further, all those pesky headlines about former detainees popping back up on the battlefield ready, willing, and able to kill American soldiers is enough to give (some) Democrats in marginal seats the (electoral) jitters. Still, Mr. Obama's determination to secure closure by the end of his tenure means only sixty-one terrorists remain behind bars.

Yet, terror recruits have multiplied during the years the prison has been winding down, and no American "cred" has been earned by the high-profile prisoner transfers. Terrorists do not need Gitmo or any other prison to hate us; they hate because we prosper in our pluralistic democracy.

Syria

Not so long ago, Mr. Obama was keen on U.S. non-intervention in Syria. But such inaction opened the door to all kinds of bad outcomes, including Russia's propping up of the brutal Assad regime through a bombing campaign against pro-Western, anti-Assad forces and the deepening of an already burgeoning refugee crisis. The war-torn country has also served as a vital recruitment venue for the Islamic State. Here, Putin's ability to fill a power vacuum bolsters Russia's Middle East presence at the same time American influence continues to wane.

China

Seems not a week passes without another incident in the South China Sea. But a panel of jurists at The Hague has recently rejected China's island-grabbing ways—a setback for an aggressive Chinese government determined to expand artificial island building in troubled waters. Few believe the panel will be able to enforce its judgment, however. And, true to form, additional provocations have followed, including the sending of Chinese warships into waters claimed by Japan.

Such aggressive action has generated little overt resistance in Southeast Asia and Europe, but ASEAN (the Association of Southeast Asian Nations) is increasingly nervous about such muscle flexing in their neighborhood.

Conclusion: Mr. Obama has proven to be the anti-Bush alright. Yet, his legacy is not "peace in our time"—but more like a reminder of what superpower passivity invites: Assad survives, ISIS proliferates, refugees flee, allies fret, and Putin is empowered. Let there be no mistake—Mr. Obama has left the world, especially the Middle East, a far more dangerous place than he found it.

Rules to Live By

December 8, 2016, *Washington Examiner*

Everybody has their favorite rules to live by. Most are instilled in us by our parents or authority figures we come to admire. My experience falls squarely within this paradigm. For example, my parents taught me to never indulge bullies. This species of reprobate is by nature insatiable: It will *always* return to collect more of your goodies where there is no penalty for doing so. Similarly, my admiration for Winston Churchill has been focused on his unwavering determination to never give in to bully bad guys—even where such belligerence was inconvenient (or worse) for his career ambitions.

These life lessons are especially relevant in geopolitics circa 2016. Just take a look at Mr. Obama's foreign policy initiatives—that collection of high-sounding, feckless policy ploys that has led to a far more dangerous world than many of us could have imagined eight years ago. And nowhere is the failure to follow the "do not indulge bullies" moral more obvious than the infamous Iranian nuclear deal.

Published news reports over the past two years reveal the U.S. either caving to Iranian interpretations of the agreement or simply adding gratuitous sweeteners to placate Tehran. These gifts include the now permissible non-disclosure of past nuclear-related scientific research, the jettisoning of "anywhere, anytime" inspections (thereby allowing the International Atomic Energy Agency to cut its own deals regarding self-inspection), a secretly negotiated side agreement to lift sanctions on Iranian state banks involved in funding its ballistic missile program, the secret airlifting of $400 million in cash (representing an initial installment of a $1.7 billion settlement) at the very moment four American prisoners were released from Iranian captivity, new guidelines to facilitate dollar transactions with Iranian businesses, and a repudiation of "snapback sanctions" should the regime be caught violating one or more of its treaty obligations.

We now know the domestic marketing of the "historic" deal was equally dubious. Recall that Ben Rhodes, Mr. Obama's alter ego, was quite willing to brag (at least until a furor over his egotistical remarks ensued) as to why it was necessary to manipulate a gullible media in order to sell the controversial deal. Also recall that the foregoing givebacks, freebies, and newly coined interpretations are at odds with numerous Obama/Kerry promises made to the American public over the past four years.

All of which begs the question of what the U.S. received in return for all of the gratuities extended to the world's leading sponsor of terror. The answer is a growing litany of provocative misdeeds— including but not limited to dangerous near-miss flybys by Iranian fighters, the detention of eleven U.S. Navy sailors by the Iranian Navy, Hezbollah's continuing murderous rampage in Syria, and the seem-ingly endless pronouncements of "Death to America" and "Death to Israel" led by Supreme Leader Khamenei—our alleged "partner" in nuclear peace.

The U.S. response to the foregoing has been sustained forbear-ance. And no close observer of Barack Obama can feign surprise at America's weak-kneed response to Iran's continuing provoca-tions. You see, the mullahs fully understand Mr. Obama was wholly invested in this "historic" deal, notwithstanding considerable Ameri-can embarrassment and continuing negative bipartisan reviews. As a result, Iran stretches, cheats, and acts out in miscreant ways because it can, without consequences.

But the U.S. election is a game changer. President-elect Trump has repeatedly stated that a high priority will be to "dismantle the disastrous deal with Iran." Yet it is far more likely that the new American president will seek to strengthen-stiffen-revisit the most problematic provisions rather than jettison the entire deal.

The primary rationale here is about keeping peace in the (allied) neighborhood. Recall our Sunni allies are more interested in a "go slow," inspection-intensive road than having to worry about a rogue neighbor fully (re)engaged in the (destabilizing) bomb building business. The "go slow" option also has the advantage of taking the bomb building pressure off the Saudis (and others similarly situated)—a strategic and economic relief to governments urgently engaged in the difficult task of economic modernization.

It was not so long ago that the Iranian economy was running on empty. Tough American sanctions and growing domestic discontent had the despotic regime on the ropes. Here, the world could get excited about the unexpected onset of a nascent democracy moment—an "Iranian spring." But the appeaser at 1600 Pennsylvania Avenue would have none of it. He wanted a foreign policy legacy deal—and he knew how to get it. Now, the Trump administration must deal with an empowered terror regime accustomed to getting its way despite repeatedly acting out in aggressive ways.

The moral in all this is indeed familiar. Mom and Dad and ole Winston got it right. In fact, Mr. Churchill said it best: "An appeaser is one who feeds a crocodile, hoping it will eat him last."

Here's hoping a new American president will secure a few pounds of flesh before further feeding.

CHAPTER 7

Progressivism's War on Speech

It would be impossible to chronicle the end of the Obama era and beginning of the Trump era without some attention given to the newest iteration of thought control on the left—the war on speech.

This topic prompts me to relate a noteworthy appearance at a GOP state party convention in Bangor, Maine, in the spring of 2016. The location was the cavernous convention hall—Cross Insurance Center. I was scheduled to address approximately 3,000 party activists during their afternoon session. There was nothing unique here except for the fact that very few attendees could have picked me out of a lineup prior to my introduction.

Many of the speeches offered that day were given by surrogates for the remaining GOP presidential hopefuls. But my talk assumed a different tone. It was not the typical "we're good; they're not" pep talk that permeates such events. My remarks were in fact focused on speech—or more precisely, the serial attacks on conservative speech (particularly on campus) during the age of Obama. The talk lasted a mere twenty minutes, but my concluding thoughts were met with an extended standing ovation. A long line waited as I arrived for a brief book signing immediately after my appearance.

The unexpected reaction gave me pause. I had not plowed new ground, but rather added meat to the bone of the various methods Obama-ites had found to either minimize conservative speech or tap additional funding streams for their own.

I've now given this talk dozens of times around the country, and still audiences are struck by the ingenuity of the left. Lois Lerner's slow-walking passive-aggressive act at the IRS was but one effective strategy. Another is the left's various "accountability" initiatives to force conservative issue advocacy groups organized as nonprofits to make public their donor/membership lists—the primary purpose of which is to intimidate or harass those who contribute to socially conservative causes such as traditional marriage or religious liberty. Also on the accountability front, recall the Soros-inspired campaign to intimidate advertisers of Rush Limbaugh and Sean Hannity, or the emotional Democratic calls for the "locality rule" or "fairness doctrine" to balance right-leaning talk radio outlets.

But these attempts to curtail speech do not compare to what community organizer groups and the Obama administration cooked up in order to sweeten the pots of social justice activists. Talk about innovative: As part of the Obama Justice Department's settlement formulas with Wall Street investment banks over the subprime mortgage meltdown (a crisis caused in part by the insistence of Congressional liberals that banks underwrite subprime loans in the first place), DOJ lawyers negotiated "volunteer" contributions from the settling banks that were in turn redirected to ACORN-like community justice groups. Worse, the banks were lured with the added incentive of double credit off their settlement obligation for every dollar so given. This was pure progressive shakedown artistry at work, as the voluntary nature of the contribution served to bypass federal law that requires settlement monies be deposited in the federal treasury.

I close my riff on these strategies with a request for all World War II veterans in the audience to stand. A few elderly soldiers struggle to their feet while acknowledging thunderous applause from the assembled. I then thank them for their service—for saving the world from Nazi totalitarianism, for allowing us to live lives of unparalleled freedom. And then, a rhetorical question: "How do you feel when you see your great-grandchildren indoctrinated with ludicrous concepts such as 'trigger warnings,' 'safe zones,' 'microaggressions,' and 'speech codes' in order to cope with...life?"

As you might imagine, the answer is none too positive. "The Greatest Generation" earned its moniker through blood, guts, and sacrifice. Eighteen-year-olds led the way, suffering immeasurable hardships to save the world. Four generations later, millennial "snowflakes" have difficulty navigating college campuses on a cloudy day. Progressives love to say their movement denotes "progress," but such behavior is anything but. This intolerance is illiberal; it mocks '60s-era liberalism and the free speech movement. It's also dangerously soft, and must be confronted and taken down at every turn.

The following columns are not soft, but more like a call to arms on behalf of warriors (right and left) who wish to take back our culture from boycott-loving, speech-hating progressives.

Whatever Happened to Free Speech?

May 12, 2016, *Washington Examiner*

A few recent media reports warrant your attention:

Item

Senator Sheldon Whitehouse, D-R.I., requests the Justice Department consider criminal charges against individuals and groups who do not share the Obama administration's views on climate change. The former U.S. attorney suggests that the Racketeer Influenced and Corrupt Organizations Act (RICO), a statute originally drafted to assist the feds in the prosecution of mafia dons and drug cartels, could serve as a legal predicate.

Item

The University of New Hampshire's "Bias-Free Language Guide" lists "problematic" words such as "mothering," "fathering," "illegal alien," "older people," "rich person," "poor person," and "Americans"—all products of hierarchy and oppression, don't you know. Alas, negative media coverage of this ludicrous project led the university to reject the proposed new speech code. Parenthetical fact: One recent study found that 55 percent of 437 alleged "institutions of higher learning" had adopted such codes.

Item

Lois Lerner and her merry band of progressive accomplices at the IRS successfully slow-played the administrative approval process for the formation of conservative nonprofits during the lead-up to the presidential election cycle of 2012. Ms. Lerner subsequently pled the Fifth when called before Congress. Alas, the 6th Circuit Court of Appeals recently required the IRS to produce the so-called "spreadsheets" it created with respect to the targeted groups.

It is difficult to miss the common thread in these stories. Indeed, such attacks on free speech are now commonplace as the Democratic Party completes its transformation from Kennedy-esque champions of freedom to progressives gone wild. Today, the chair of the Democratic National Committee finds it difficult to distinguish "Democrat" from "Socialist." Herein are those who truly "feel the Bern."

Yet, the majority of Americans who remain immune to progressivism's appeal see little more than an illiberal attack on free speech. And the mounting outrage should not be confined to dues-paying members of the "Vast Right-Wing Conspiracy, LLC."

I'm referring to so many of my slightly older friends who qualify as proud '60s liberals. These folks came of age during Kent State and the assassinations of Robert Kennedy and Martin Luther King. Some protested the war. Others marched for civil rights. Still others organized for women's equality. Such were the great social movements of the era. These dissenters changed the course of American history—and culture. And they accomplished their goals by wrapping their discontent around the First Amendment and our precious right to free speech.

Now, fast-forward to our present world, wherein the children and grandchildren of this protest-proud generation demand speech codes and trigger warnings and safe zones on their college campuses—all in order to limit speech. They disinvite speakers to campus when such invitees are deemed not pure enough for their politically correct, offense-less world. They even take over the offices of university presidents—and then demand no consequences. Their collegiate enablers are no doubt proud. Where else could they perpetuate such transparently silly constructs? Where else could they find and influence such gullible children? Where else could they find employment (even tenure) while advancing such ludicrous propositions?

Back in the real world, where the private sector has yet to establish criticism-free safe zones for overly sensitive, underperforming employees, we have a problem: how to combat progressivism's distaste for robust debate and uncomfortable dissent.

The obvious answer is to elect a president who does not subscribe to the rules of political correctness; a leader who is ready, willing, and able to remind the wider culture that our unique experiment in democracy and freedom is all about protest and dissent. In other words, let's go old school and shame 'em. Make 'em take a course in U.S. history, join a debating society, read (and understand) Dr. King's speeches, maybe even research *The Federalist Papers*.

Admittedly, this "tough love" approach is radical. Requiring college students to read, write, and think about their freedoms would generate Congressional investigations and widespread campus demonstrations. The ACLU would be brought in to stop the exercise. And I don't want to think about the depth and variety of trigger warnings such learning would set off in the minds of so many coddled students.

Memo to the voting public: What a few years ago was unthinkable (even laughable) on our college campuses is today a primary tool for those who wish to fundamentally transform America and limit our cherished right to free—even provocative—speech.

Those of us who reject such dangerous cultural revisionism possess the means to reverse course. The family dinner table at semester break is a good place to start. But the message must originate from the top—from the Oval Office. Our path to this realigning freedom begins on November 8, 2016.

To Boycott or Not to Boycott

February 16, 2017, *Washington Examiner*

I have a tough one for all of you with reasonable minds and conservative bents. The issue at hand is how to react to the seemingly unlimited iterations of protests and boycotts unleashed by the left since life as they knew it changed during the early evening hours of November 8.

First, a point of historical context: Boycotts are not new to politics; they are a primary tool for those seeking social change. History records that both sides utilized such weapons to great effect in the decades-running fight for civil rights. Segregationists wielded it as a punishment against those who advocated for integration. But it was Martin Luther King Jr and the NAACP that turned these tactics into a truly effective strategy in the battle against those who refused to recognize basic civil rights for black Americans. In the process, a Woolworth's lunch counter in Greensboro, North Carolina, became "boycott central" for the civil rights movement.

Now fast-forward to the Obama era. The election of Barack Obama gave rise to a multitude of boycott-involved campaigns—all of them checking one or more boxes on the progressive playlist. These included organized protests and/or boycotts of talk radio advertisers, the Koch brothers, Chick-fil-A, Hobby Lobby—even a boycott of an entire state (North Carolina) for its adoption of a transgender bathroom bill.

Today, no venue is too small for the supposedly tolerant but now always aggrieved left. A case in point is Goldberg's New York Bagels, a small kosher eatery located in deep blue Pikesville, Maryland. Goldberg's owner, Stanley Drebin, saw a 15 percent loss in business once he expressed support for Donald Trump in the weeks leading up to the presidential election. In a familiar refrain, lefties used Facebook to call for a boycott.

More often than not, boycotts *work* (Chick-fil-A being an exception) as well-organized groups with serious economic firepower tend to carry the day. No surprise here: The party of community organizers really knows how to organize against free speech.

On the other side of the aisle, conservatives tend to focus on... position letters and white papers. The political right just doesn't do boycotts very well—or often.

Think about it. Have you ever heard of a conservative boycott of San Francisco—Berkeley—Harvard—an Elizabeth Warren speech—or *The New York Times*? Do riots break out at Liberty University when a liberal is invited to campus? Have you ever read of Young Republicans storming the office of a university president and demanding... an end to grade inflation or the elimination of campus "safe zones"?

But the Trump era has now arrived. And the question of how a conservative is to conduct himself in the age of Trump presents a unique challenge. Certainly, frustration over Obama-era political correctness and the unleashed energy of the deplorables has made many on the right edgy. They're lookin' for a fight—or maybe a boycott or two.

The internet age makes supporting information easily accessible. On the right, groups such as Second Vote rate corporations and organizations on the basis of their support for conservative-leaning positions, such as gun rights, immigration, religious liberty, etc. Similar websites exist on the left and are targeted to usual suspects such as talk radio, Fox News, oil companies, the NRA, and now, of course, L.L. Bean. But lefty boycotts are "dog bites man"—expected, so Obama-era...not "new" news.

Which brings us back to the conservative's dilemma. You could choose to target actors: (Sarandon, DiCaprio, Fonda), a Broadway play (*Hamilton*), your morning latte (Starbucks), your least favorite NFL quarterback (Kaepernick), or the best three-point shooter in the league (Curry), among thousands of other options. On the other hand, you might go with a positive option by doubling down on the people and businesses that support *your* views. This option could be fun—you could indulge that extra chicken sandwich, a Tom Brady football, or attend as many Gary Sinise movies as humanly possible. In Pikesville, it would mean an extra dozen bagels from your favorite deli. (Goldberg's has seen a recent uptick in orders from around the country[!] since calls for the boycott made national news.)

This (happy) option is even more attractive given the events of the past month. Think about it: You can "Eat more chikin," watch more Jon Voight movies, even listen to more Zac Brown songs, while your progressive "friends" carry angry signs, shout angry chants, march in angry parades, spread angry fake news, and eat inferior bagels—and all because they didn't get their way on November 8.

The bottom line should be clear. Use your time and money to support the good guys. Feel the positive vibes rather than copy the left's dated boycotts. (Okay, maybe make one exception for ole "Hanoi Jane" in honor of my U.S. Marine dad.)

So, what about you? Which road will you take in response to the relentless shenanigans demonstrated daily and ad nauseam by progressive snowflakes on the other side?

Volunteerism, Obama Style

March 16, 2017, *Washington Examiner*

My former Congressional seat was what Washington pundits call "safe." It means that the district's boundaries were drawn to the specifications of a particular political party—and viewpoint.

Such seats typically guarantee re-election in the absence of scandal. Still, local unions unhappy with my votes would from time to time picket my office, if just to remind me they were watching. A minor annoyance, yes, but nevertheless one I wanted to repay. And so one day my campaign staff greeted the protest line with notes attached to a brown-bag lunch—the greeting read in part that the assembled should eat up, because it was the last free lunch coming their way. The participants were not amused.

I was reminded of this story in the aftermath of my recent appearance on MSNBC wherein I stated numerous anti-Trump protests so heavily covered by the mainstream press were organized efforts by well-heeled progressive groups with paid staffs. The notion of paid protesters set my fellow panelists off. "Not amused" does not do their attitude justice; "indignant" probably best describes the reaction. After all, the left can't adhere to their favorite adjective ("organic") if the protests are being funded by organized activists—or can they?

Well, they can certainly try. But anyone who cares to educate themselves on the ways and means of the protester class will quickly uncover a well-financed, comprehensive plan of civil unrest sponsored by some varsity players in the world of community agitating and organizing.

The movement is led by "Organizing for Action"—a progeny of President Barack Obama's first presidential campaign. Closely aligned with OFA is the recently activated "Indivisible Project," led by co-founder Angel Padilla, an analyst at the National Immigration

Law Center. The Center is a beneficiary of the George Soros–funded Open Society Foundations.

OFA and Indivisible are credited with the recent "spontaneous" protests at (Republican) town hall meetings around the country. You have no doubt seen media reports of the disruptive crowds and loud chants. They're not exactly focused on a substantive give-and-take with the local Members of Congress. Rather, they are more like what millennial lefties are trained to do on college campuses—just shout the opposition down. The association with Obama makes these outfits "grievance central," certain to be in the vanguard of the dissident movement going forward.

"Indivisible" specializes in online training for the protester class— sorta like a University of Phoenix for left-wing activists. It was begun by former Democratic Congressional staffers especially aggrieved by Hillary Clinton's defeat. Its "guide" is targeted to equally upset activists who are willing to transform traditional question-and-answer town halls into resistance platforms on behalf of progressive causes.

None of this should be a surprise to those familiar with the ways and means of Capitol Hill politics. One of my earliest memories as a new member of the House Banking Committee was an ACORN-sponsored demonstration at one of our public hearings. At the time, ACORN was all about the business of leveraging subprime loans from local banks—institutions that required a passing CRA ("Community Reinvestment Act") rating in order to grow. Banks that failed to indulge the subprime agenda would become the target of organized protest. You will recall what eventually happened to all those bad loans that were underwritten and subsequently wrapped into mortgage products sold to the world. Obama called it "the worst financial crisis since the Great Depression." He was correct, but failed to note that political pressure to underwrite questionable loans was a major cause of the crisis. Alas, no politician made the list of those most responsible for our historic mortgage crisis and recession.

Many liberals believed that Washington's progressive agenda would keep on chugging down the line for another eight years—until the evening of November 8 hit real hard. Suddenly, the party was over. Momentum was lost. The agenda was placed on indefinite hold.

All this has, in turn, led to plenty of angry Americans exercising their right to take it to the streets. No problem there. Protests are as All-American as apple pie and American exceptionalism. But a brief reminder to those engaged in what is a very public exercise of their First Amendment rights: Don't tell us all of this activity is spontaneous, or that the Soros-sponsored usual suspects aren't footing the bill. The dots are not that difficult to connect. And besides, we know there is no such thing as a free lunch.

How to Restore the First Amendment on Campus

May 11, 2017, *Washington Examiner*

There has been plenty of recent analysis devoted to today's age of rage on campus. Much of it focuses on the left's reaction to Trump-style populism. But I have been writing about the ways, means, and ends of this dangerous phenomenon for much of the past decade. Herewith are five takeaways for your consideration.

1. Progressives delegitimize rather than oppose dissenting views.

Adults understand the mere rendering of political opinion (whether right or left) does not constitute a personal threat or present a dangerous environment to the listener. This is commonsense stuff, but unacceptable to those who are in the business of degrading opposing views. These folks magnify the meaning of "harassment" or "threat" by claiming that even socially acceptable opposing opinions create such a hostile environment that they feel physically threatened—and in need of refuge (i.e., a safe zone). Here, opinions at odds with progressive doctrine are molded into hostile acts. Accordingly, "I watch Fox" or "I oppose racial quotas" or "I believe in traditional marriage" or "I oppose women in combat" are deemed qualifying aggressive actions. The accompanying loss of intellectual curiosity and intellectual engagement is not seen as problematic for campus practitioners and their faculty enablers. This magnification process has led to many ludicrous yet widely reported cases of harassment on campus.

2. The most severe strain of this theology legitimizes violence as an acceptable response.

You may have seen interviews with defenders of campus violence over the past year. Their intellectual argument (such as it is) follows a familiar path: because the words employed by the offender are deemed threatening to the recipient, he/she *has* no choice but to lash out at the offender. The irony of college students screaming "Nazi!" or "fascist!" while demonstrating in violent (often criminal) ways seems lost on the afflicted. Note that even the Berkeley police department buys into this fiction. These supposed keepers of the peace are instructed to intervene in campus protests only when the threat of imminent physical harm is at issue; mere property damage rampages do not qualify. In other words, good luck to you and your nice new car on the Berkeley campus.

3. Few progressives see their provocative actions as antithetical to traditions of free speech.

I often ask my '60s-generation friends to compare their social activism with today's campus contrarians. Most are unimpressed with the current crowd. No surprise here. The great cultural movements of that era (women's, civil rights, anti-war) were all about dissent and protest—sometimes crossing the line into civil disobedience. Indeed, it was during this time that Berkeley became the "home" of the free speech movement. Fifty years later, it has become home to lawlessness and illiberal demands for the silencing of alternative opinion. What could be more damaging to speech than uninviting conservative speakers to campus or shouting them down once they get there?

4. Post-grad snowflakes are in a world of hurt.

There is not much data devoted to what occurs when progressive millennials graduate from their isolation zones and are forced to deal with post-graduation reality. And I don't mean graduate school. I'm talking about the real world—the one where you either sink or swim in the private marketplace—where missing work, in order to demonstrate against some real or perceived social injustice, is decidedly not cool.

Some difficult questions come to mind: Do sit-ins follow the realization that there are no safe zones in the graduate's new workplace?

To whom do you send the endless list of microaggressions perpetrated on you by your insensitive, mean boss? How to deal with one's "feelings" after suffering the slings and arrows of a poor job review? Where do underperforming employees go to feel better about themselves?

Of course, the lefty administrators and professors who have executed this PC hoax on impressionable young minds have no such problems. They did their job—just punched the clock and turned out a whole new generation of victims and social justice warriors. But millennials should not expect them to engage in private-sector protests as they tend to stay safely ensconced in their tenure-protected ivory towers. Just doesn't seem fair...

5. What to do?

Numerous conservative pundits have urged the new administration to withhold federal funds from schools that serially fail to protect First Amendment rights. (The feds already have the power to withhold dollars from institutions that violate anti-discrimination laws.) We can only hope Mr. Trump will wield his big stick in support of speech.

A tough-minded response is required because our unfortunate cultural experiment in too many participation trophies (and far too little parental guidance) has backfired. The resulting generation of overprotected and self-absorbed adolescents is ill-prepared for life's myriad challenges and disappointments. Many of these same students "feel the Bern" because life is so unfair and because "Democratic socialism" sounds so cool. Lost in the process has been learning, social engagement, critical thinking, and personal growth—at $50,000 a year to boot.

Ironically, the same institutions of higher learning that have presided over this silliness will soon be hitting you, parents and alumni, up for your annual giving contribution. A portion of this money will be used to pay the salaries of arrogant elitists who preach illiberal, hateful lessons about...*you.* Here's a thought: Maybe you should see that annual giving solicitation as your very own microaggression, and just say "no."

These Days, Religious Liberty Is Sitting Pretty in Church

June 1, 2017, *Washington Examiner*

A life in politics means regular visits to churches, synagogues, mosques, or any combination of houses of worship. Such occasions convey a sense of respect for the institution and people of faith. An aspiring candidate's presence is often recognized from the pulpit. Whether anything other than mere recognition occurs depends upon the officiant. In rare cases, an invitation will be extended to say a few words or shake hands with the congregation while they file out. Suffice it to say much can be riding on such appearances.

I've been thinking of my many hours spent in places of worship (while on the campaign trail) as the issue of religious liberty again re-emerges—but now with a far different perspective from the one applied during President Barack Obama's administration.

The news item at the heart of the latest upheaval is President Trump's recent executive order aimed at circumscribing the so-called "Johnson Amendment," thereby instructing the IRS to give wide latitude to charitable organizations, including clergy, while monitoring speech in (tax-exempt) places of worship. Despite a bit of mild criticism from the right as to how the president's instruction could have utilized stronger verbiage, the expanded berth is nevertheless a positive development. Nobody really knew where the Johnson Amendment's line between free speech and political activism actually fell, which led to legitimate concerns about (selective) enforcement. Here, people could rightfully be concerned about a powerful federal agency exercising discretion over highly protected speech.

Unsurprisingly, this latest order has drawn howls of protest from the usual suspects—secular progressives practiced in the art of "howling." But there is a deeper reason for their angst. A new sheriff named Trump seems intent on reversing Obama-era limitations on religious liberty. And there are far more consequential issues in the pipeline than whether the local congressman gave greetings from the pulpit last Sunday.

A first step is Trump's demonstrated enthusiasm for remaking the American judiciary—a campaign commitment the administration seems intent on keeping. Today, reliably liberal Obama appointees make up approximately 40 percent of the federal judiciary. In response, the president is taking dead aim at the approximately 120 vacancies in the federal district and circuit courts. It is the stuff of recurring nightmares for progressives: a generation of younger, conservative judges intent on interpreting rather than inventing the law *and* unenthusiastic about the progressive push to punish or ban offensive (read: not politically correct) speech. Indeed, despite all the manufactured mudslinging around the nomination of Neil Gorsuch, our new Supreme Court justice was simply the opening act in what is planned to be a sustained campaign in support of judicial restraint and free speech.

Another prominent liberty issue is conscience clause protection, until recently a demilitarized zone in the contemporary culture wars. Indeed, the ability of religiously affiliated health care providers to follow their faith-based principles was (not so long ago) well recognized by both sides of the abortion divide. I can even recall a time (the early 1990s) when the overwhelming pro-choice legislature of deep blue Maryland (of which I was a member) included comprehensive conscience clause protection while passing the most pro-choice statute in the country.

But things changed dramatically during the uber-progressive Obama era. Some of you may remember Obama's visit to Notre Dame wherein he promised the assembled that his administration would continue to honor conscience clause protections. A few years later, Obama's Justice Department sued the Little Sisters of the Poor for refusing to pay for insurance coverage that included abortion services.

The most recent class of religious liberty cases focuses on the freedom of commercial vendors to decline participation in gay weddings.

Early cases focused on wedding cakes and photography services. Similar commercial settings will invariably arise in the future. In addition to the usual emotionalism of the respective sides, herein is a consequential clash of fundamental rights: the right to marry (and the right to purchase related goods and services) against the individual vendor's right to religious liberty in the secular space. Obama's Justice Department predictably took a limited view of religious liberty rights in such circumstances. A Jeff Sessions–led Department of Justice is likely to adopt a more expansive posture.

Next up in our cultural parade of rights will be issues relative to transgender individuals—from the bathroom to the classroom to adoption services. And who knows the next generation's (civil rights) cause of choice. But a new president has begun to change the dialogue and the legal playing field. Henceforth, expressions of religious conviction will receive added protection, as will the under-reported plight of persecuted Christians around the world.

The bottom line: Executive branch control under Trump gives conservatives the power to influence cultural debates similar to the way progressives exerted their influence during the Obama years.

All of which means plenty of acrimony, protests, and litigation going forward.

A Letter to My Son, as He Prepares to Start College in a Time of Campus Craziness

June 22, 2017, *Washington Examiner*

Congratulations, son! Your high school graduation is now in the books. Lifelong friends, favorite teachers, and big wins (and losses) will define these formative years.

But now a new cycle begins. College life awaits. Plenty of new challenges will be presented—academically, socially, athletically, and...politically. With respect to the first three of these, you have demonstrated an ability to handle your business. Here, your brains, brawn, and common sense have served you well. Such attributes will continue to serve you in your new environment.

The fourth challenge will be somewhat unique, however. Some of your new peers (and professors) will seek to define (and degrade) you by the fact that your parents earn a good living; you are the product of a two-parent home; you attended excellent private schools; you are a Christian; you are a white male; you are a Republican; you are a conservative.

Your spiritual upbringing has taught you that all of this does not for a second make you better, or worse, than any other person on this earth. You have often heard Mom and me talk about judging others according to their values, actions, character—rather than the color of their skin (or any other characteristic for that matter). This is what Dr. Martin Luther King was referring to in his famous "I Have a Dream" speech. It remains advice for the ages.

But today's college environment seeks to question even this most basic of values. You see, there is a new, virulent ideology bumping around "higher" education and, therefore, our culture. It is called "identity politics"—a brand of progressive thought that has gained an unfortunate foothold with your generation, and is especially popular on campus.

This platform turns King's advice on its head. It seeks to impose judgment as a function of everything but personal character. And people that look like you and have your kind of background will often find themselves in its crosshairs.

This means that you must be prepared to deal with those who will label you in order to denigrate you. The more aggressive types will tag you with the "product of privilege" moniker. This means you will be identified as a "hater"—an unfeeling type incapable of empathizing with the plight of those less fortunate—defined as just about everyone who does not fit your description.

This, of course, is the essence of identity politics. It is also a first-class, in-your-face guilt trip that may also be administered by professors and administrators who just live for this stuff.

Recent years have brought us the most radical iteration of this "movement." It unfolds almost daily on our television screens during commencement season—or whenever a conservative speaker appears on a left-wing campus.

The scenes capture aggressively violent young people acting out in order to shut down or intimidate the audience and speaker. Sometimes, the protesters are heard screaming expletives such as "fascist!" or "Nazi!" They also tend to carry signs, lots of signs, with every "victim" cause known to mankind. The riots at Berkeley and Middlebury have been the most grotesque, but many campuses have experienced this sickening intolerance.

The election of President Trump has given these snowflake-protesters a convenient boogeyman to hate; but truth be told, they did not need a disrupter such as Trump to come along in order to strut their stuff. This group believes they own the moral high ground because of their self-identified victimhood. And those like you, my dear son, are the designated victimizers, aka "oppressors." Yes, you and your ilk are "The Man"—just grinding various victim groups down for your own nativist, racist, homophobic, capitalist purposes—or so the popular narrative goes.

And please do not let the fact that so many of these "oppressed" young people come from wealthy, private-school backgrounds confuse you. The guilt that accompanies their economic advantage only makes them angrier.

Today, this mindset has infiltrated the Democratic Party to its core. Conservative Democrats have been vaporized. Moderates have been shuttered. The party's once consequential block of right-of-center "Blue Dogs" is on life support.

And all in the name of political correctness.

The left-wing intelligentsia (yes, the same group that gave us modern victimology) has now morphed into the go-to advisory group for the "The Resistance." In this capacity, progressive pundits are providing advice on how best to talk to the great unwashed, i.e., "deplorables" who somehow ended up voting for Trump. People like...us.

Your job is not to go looking for conflict with campus progressives. But if conflict does find you, you know not to back down. In this context, engage where you can and debate with substance when opposing remarks dignify a response. If possible, remind the opposition millennials that college is (still) supposed to be about the respectful exchange of ideas.

But never allow them to shut you down. Bad things happen when good people are silenced. Never allow yourself to be silenced.

And call your mother!

Love,

Dad

Is Charlottesville the Beginning of the End of Trump?

August 23, 2017, *Washington Examiner*

Fact

"We condemn in the strongest possible terms this egregious display of hatred, bigotry, and violence on many sides. On many sides. It's been going on for a long time in our country. Not Donald Trump, not Barack Obama, this has been going on for a very long time.

Our country is doing very well in so many ways....We have unemployment the lowest it has been in seventeen years. We have companies pouring into our country. Car companies and so many others, they're coming back into our country. We are renegotiating trade deals to make them great for [our] country and great for the American worker. We have so many incredible things happening in our country.

So when I watch Charlottesville, to me, it's very, very sad."

Opinion

Someone at the White House figured out rather quickly that this was an insufficient response. Hence, a quick background follow-up by a White House staffer assured the country that the president was "condemning hatred, bigotry, and violence from all sources and all sides..." There followed two additional statements of condemnation, only one of which was deemed by pundits to be suitably strong enough. The media made sure the response would be joined with a similar lukewarm reaction in the aftermath of former Ku Klux Klan leader David Duke's attempted endorsement of candidate Trump in February 2016.

Two of the three Charlottesville responses missed their mark—for no good reason. Condemnation of assorted neo-Nazi-affiliated racist groups is by no means heavy lifting, but must be strong and unequivocal. Gratuitous observations regarding the presence of leftist radicals or the importance of acknowledging (rather than destroying) history may be accurate, but are best left unsaid when unadulterated evil is at issue.

A primary consequence is to encourage an already enflamed media to supersize its favorite new storyline (at least since the gradual demise of the Trump/Russian collusion story): the rise of the Trump-aligned alt-right. This narrative is especially dangerous in that it allows the pasting of fringe racist organizations onto the Trump base, thereby demeaning millions of regular old working-class Republicans and Democrats who have legitimate concerns about jobs, border control, sanctuary cities, and an increasingly permissive culture. (Of course, it delegitimizes the president as well.)

To borrow a phrase, the media seeks to degrade "Pittsburgh, not Paris"—what remains a mysterious land for lefty pundits. How these good folks take to being lumped in with social misfits and à la carte racists will be interesting to watch. You may recall Hillary Clinton's "deplorables" label didn't sit very well with this crowd. They let her know of their disapproval last November.

Fact

President Trump's approval rating has settled around 40 percent, with disapproval in the mid-50s. But neither Chuck Schumer nor Nancy Pelosi (with approval numbers in the mid-30s) is able to take political advantage.

Opinion

Trump hate will fuel the Democratic base in 2018. Democrats will likely pick up seats, as the out-of-power party typically performs well in midterm elections. But it is going to be difficult to sustain momentum with its present agenda and cast of (leadership) characters. Sensitivity to identity politics requires Democratic leaders parrot the progressive line, without exception.

Yet a platform of higher taxes, single-payer health care, open borders, sanctuary cities, abortion on demand, a war on fossil fuels, and multiculturalism is not a formula for success between the coasts. To make matters worse, a significantly reduced "Blue Dog" caucus is nowhere to be found and seems unable to "right" the ship.

Fact

The RNC raised $75.4 million in the first six months of 2017 compared to the DNC's $38.2 million. The RNC also reported 11 million more small donors (defined as less than $200 contributors) than the DNC and had six times more cash on hand ($45 million to $7.5 million).

Opinion

Under normal circumstances, these numbers would be status quo. The president's party always attracts significant dollars—cash follows power and all that.

But this is the age of Trump. Nothing is normal. Many pundits believed the president's diminishing poll numbers would have at least slowed down the GOP money train. That does not appear to be the case, at least not yet.

Maybe we should not be surprised. Trump has been able to navigate seriously negative stories and near-death political experiences better than any politician in memory. Whether Charlottesville and its aftermath is simply an add-on to a long list of close calls or a real turning point against Trump will be made clearer on the first Tuesday of November 2018. But the July–December 2017 fundraising reports will give us an early clue.

Ehrlich on Trump and the NFL: Penalties on All Sides

September 29, 2017, *The Baltimore Sun*

My then nine-year-old sandlot-playing son, Drew, was once quoted by a reporter as saying, "Football is life." That about says all you need to know about football and the Ehrlichs. Indeed, the sport was my ticket to life success—a path that Drew (now eighteen and a strong safety at Villanova) and thirteen-year-old Josh (a quarterback for Drew's former sandlot team) are eager to follow.

What, then, to make of all the controversy of athletes kneeling during the national anthem and the emotional response of the fans who have made the sport America's favorite? It seems everyone wants to add their two cents to the discussion. Here are mine.

Most will recall that the foundation for the anthem kneeling exercise was Colin Kaepernick's social justice protest regarding racial inequality and especially police brutality directed at African Americans. (Some will also recall the cop/pig socks he wore at practice, just in case you did not know how the young quarterback views our men and women in blue.) Of course, the evidence is far from settled regarding this favorite progressive narrative. In fact, the raw data do not support a systematic police campaign to murder African Americans. But why let facts get in the way of a progressive political agenda intended to fuel division and civil unrest?

Of course, there are instances of police brutality and African American victims; in some of these cases the defendant policemen have wrongfully escaped punishment. Here, issues of police negligence are real—as are the tensions in many black communities where police relations are always tenuous. In other cases, such as Michael Brown in Ferguson, Missouri, and Freddie Gray in Baltimore, the facts do not support the indictment. Still, some continue to perpetuate the unsupported storylines. Such is life in the race industry—no relation to the praiseworthy civil rights movement that will forever be led by Rev. Martin Luther King and his genuinely wonderful dream.

The Kaepernick-induced wounds were still bleeding when the president chipped in with his incendiary wish that NFL owners "fire" those "sons of b—s" who chose to kneel. That in turn generated further response last weekend when many more players joined in the kneeling. A portion of our football-loving nation interpreted this as an exercise in protected political speech in the great American tradition; others viewed it as spoiled millionaire athletes degrading the flag and country—and on an international stage to boot (see Jaguars/Ravens in London). The irony of U.S. citizens kneeling for the anthem while standing for "God Save the Queen" (in a country once known for its empire) was not lost on many observers. All of which requires me to throw a flag on all three parties.

First, I, along with many Republicans, was sometimes critical of President Barack Obama's habit of opining on issues large—but also *small*. I repeat my criticism herein: President Donald Trump is on the precipice of a historic tax reform that could jump-start economic growth missing for the last decade. He is also engaged in a war of words with an unstable, saber-rattling nuclear dictator in North Korea—and all the while dealing with our federal government's response to the devastating natural disasters that have hit Texas, Florida, and Puerto Rico. He (and we) do not need the added drama of the NFL clumsily scrambling to protect its brand.

Fifteen yards must also be assessed against the players. I understand their displeasure at being targeted by a polarizing president, but few in America enjoy unlimited freedom of expression in the workplace. Accordingly, those who insist on making political statements "at the office" should not be surprised at the emotional responses that ensue. One more thing: Many would feel better about the player protesters if they had either done something to stop the killing of so many innocent people in our poorest neighborhoods or shown appropriate empathy for the families of fallen police officers—our first line of defense when riots erupt and cities burn.

A game misconduct penalty also goes to the NFL. They have allowed the player protests on the field to (no pun intended) trump the game. It is a league that seems more interested in the length of a player's sock than the fact that millions of its customers are upset with what they perceive as disrespect for a country that has made so many owners and players wealthy beyond their wildest expectations. It is also a league more than mildly inconsistent on speech. Recall last year's attempt by the Cowboys to wear a helmet decal in support of Dallas police after the murder of five officers. (Ironically, the decal read "Arm in Arm.") The NFL denied the request.

A final word on race or, more specifically, the terrible pejorative "racist," for my friends on the progressive left. The little boy who cried wolf has nothing on you. The record speaks for itself: welfare reform—"racist!"; charter schools—"racist!"; photo ID at the polls—"racist!"; Western civilization—"racist!"; opposition to a $15 minimum wage—"racist!"; immigration enforcement—"racist!"; a border wall—"racist!"; English as our official language—"racist!" Thanks to you, people of goodwill but opposing viewpoints now tend to shut down—who needs the abuse? Thanks to you, a once overwhelmingly powerful accusation has lost its impact. You will only have yourselves to blame when real racism rears its ugly head—and people just yawn.

Things are now spiraling out of control. NFL TV ratings are down. Stadium attendance is down. Jersey/season ticket burnings on social media are regular occurrences around the country. Damage control is in full swing—but may be too little too late. Some players are backing down; others are doubling down. Many, no doubt, wish the entire thing would just go away.

Here's an idea. The league and Players Association agree to fund and host interactive gatherings of police and kids from the poorest of neighborhoods on a regular basis. Maybe even fund new Police

Athletic Leagues for young people born into deep poverty. Such action would lower the temperature. Encourage interaction. Give voice to legitimate community concerns. Humanize the police. It's worth a try. Oh, and everybody stands for the anthem. Like it or not, it represents the perfect vision of an imperfect people.

Out-of-Touch Kneeling NFL Players Are Starting to Ruin Emotional Attachment to Football

October 15, 2017, *Washington Examiner*

Natural and manmade tragedies in Houston, Florida, Puerto Rico, and Las Vegas have diverted public attention from NFL protests. Indeed, the magnitude of human suffering associated with historic storms and the worst mass shooting in U.S. history has again reminded us of what really counts in life.

But the controversy lives. Some players continue to kneel. Many fans continue to boo. Advertisers continue to fret. The NFL continues to search for compromise. And all "sides" continue to talk past one another, a surefire formula for continuing ill feelings.

Colin Kaepernick's original decision to take a knee was a direct response to police shootings of African Americans. We know this because Kaepernick said so. Immediately thereafter and continuing to this very day, however, the police indictment has been enlarged to include a more general critique of the criminal justice system's treatment of African Americans. We know this because many of the kneeling players have said so.

That the former charge rests on thin evidence is a matter of fact. Despite a persistent media narrative to the contrary, the statistics (as compiled by *The Washington Post* and various other media sources, as well as the federal government) show that police killings and brutalizations of African Americans are quite rare. Infrequent but highly sensationalized exceptions do not prove the rule.

With regard to the latter, troublesome facts abound. A disproportionate number of African American children are raised in poor households. Fatherlessness continues to be endemic (much as it is for poor white children). And far too many minority kids raised in deep poverty are sentenced to dysfunctional public schools, schools that fail them. As a result, African American children are over-represented in the juvenile and adult correctional systems. These are uncontroverted facts and deserving of serious debate regardless of one's political affiliation.

The incarceration statistics are an intolerable reality in a nation of unparalleled wealth. Accordingly, players who wish to utilize an appropriate public platform in order to articulate their concerns (and engage the public) about these issues will find plenty of fans willing to listen.

But players need to listen too. An overwhelming majority of Americans view the flag and anthem as symbols of freedom, sacrifice, and opportunity, cherished values albeit pursued by an imperfect country and people. Here, fans do not interpret the kneeling as an exercise in speech, but rather a very public snub aimed at unifying symbols. The bottom line: Far too many Americans have fought, bled, and died with that flag on their shoulder. No amount of "but we didn't mean to disrespect the flag" disclaimers will erase the image of kneeling players.

If you doubt this observation, consider the Baltimore Ravens' pre-anthem "ceremony" at M&T Bank Stadium on October 1. Stadium announcer Bruce Cunningham informed the crowd that players and coaches alike would take a knee prior to the anthem in prayer for "unity, kindness, and justice for all Americans." The fans still booed. And, trust me, they were not booing justice or the prayer. They were booing a compromise that pleased few; they will continue to boo any kneeling activity around the flag and country. That many players expressed shock over the adverse reaction from fans speaks to how out of touch they are when it comes to the average fan experience.

Fallout from all the controversy is a mixed bag. Most fans will continue to pay for their private seat licenses and attend games. Player jerseys will continue to be seen around NFL stadiums. Millions will continue to watch their favorite teams on television.

But the league has taken a hit. Lower TV ratings and increased numbers of no-shows at games are objective measures of real damage inflicted.

But there is another negative form of fan reaction as well. And this one is more difficult to quantify.

It's about ratcheting back one's emotional attachment. After all, such attachment is the currency for any athletic enterprise. It is what makes you look forward to Sunday afternoons, and what brings you joy or depression at the final gun. In tangible terms, it concerns whether fans will continue to rearrange their lives in order to accommodate professional football. That this decision has become a close call for a percentage of the paying customers spells trouble for a wildly successful commercial operation that was, until recent years, the proverbial goose that laid the golden egg. The size of future eggs will depend on whether all parties to the matter are able to lower the temperature and begin to listen to each other.

The gambler in me would probably take the "under" on that one.

CHAPTER 8

Can't Stop Laughing

Humor is the great disarming tool of politics. Two of our most beloved modern presidents (Kennedy and Reagan) used it to great effect. These leaders understood how difficult it is to dislike a politician while that same politician is making one laugh out loud. Their humor was often a self-deprecating brand that reflected a sense of humility—from the leader of the free world.

Today, the use of humor as a successful strategy is far less common. Unfortunately, our recent commanders-in-chief lacked the comic timing required of funny politicians (although Mr. Obama could make the grade on occasion).

But America's rapidly changing culture has also played a part. The advent of a wide-ranging political correctness (and accompanying victim identity) is the primary culprit. This new social and rhetorical arrangement makes it far more difficult to poke fun at gender, ethnicity, race, or even socioeconomic class because so many have been awarded "victim" status—with the exception of conservatives and Christians—since it is these "entitled" groups that allegedly produced all the "victims" in the first place.

One response is to boycott what had previously been accommodating venues, such as colleges and universities. This is the option comedians Jerry Seinfeld and Chris Rock took in deciding to decline further campus gigs. Their rationale: The grief from the PC police was just not worth the effort. After all, what comedian wants to watch his or her words for fear of offense or reprisal?

Another option is to take progressive agenda items to their [il]logical extreme. This is the course of action I have chosen over the years of my politics and writing. It is great fun. One *never* runs out of topics to analyze, as there is an unlimited supply of lunacy from "snowflake" millennials and their adult enablers. Indeed, "Trump derangement syndrome" (not my coinage, but Charles Krauthammer's) has penetrated the collective consciousness of the left to a depth only matched during the early days of the Reagan administration. Don't believe me? Don't believe things are that far out of control on the left flank? Well, take a look at these scary news reports from the future.

Take This Test

September 29, 2016, *Washington Examiner*

At times, life after politics can sure include plenty of...politics. I have only myself to blame. Public speaking, books, and media appearances guarantee that politically involved folks will continue to volunteer their opinions—whether invited or not. Yet, I find many of the opinion givers are confused about politics, politicians, and especially policy. Three years ago, these fascinating (if frustrating) conversations led me to publish a column that attempted to assist the politically overwhelmed as to their appropriate party identification. The piece was a hit, not least because it got a whole bunch of people to come up with their own political identity quiz, a fun pastime for political junkies in an election year. (I included this column in a humor chapter of my book, *Turning Point*.)

Alas, 2016 brings more angst to the politically involved than we have seen for quite some time. Some Republicans continue to fret over Donald Trump's sometimes coarse, always unorthodox methods. It's *The Art of the Deal* brought to big-time politics. But many of the reviews are less than glowing—just too far out of the box for traditional GOP consumption. In fact, a number of high-profile GOPers remain unimpressed with "The Donald." More than a few may end up voting Libertarian in November.

On the other side of the aisle, another Clinton with a seemingly endless set of real-life scandals (but far less charm) has emerged. She maintains a narrow lead in most polls, despite the fact that more than half the voters believe she is a compulsive liar—seemingly unable to recognize truth from fiction—whether pertaining to matters of state or her own health.

The result (to date) has been a highly polarized campaign remarkably free of substantial debate but heavy on personal attacks.

Accordingly, polls show a high degree of dissatisfaction with both major party candidates.

These cross-currents can mean only one thing: It is time for an updated quiz on behalf of the politically challenged—circa 2016. And so the following is presented for your political edification—and amusement. Hope you enjoy.

The New Party Identification Test

Select one option from each column in each section.

Progressive Insurance	Elephant Insurance
Colin Kaepernick	Roger Staubach
Ben & Jerry's	Chick-fil-A
Workplace violence	Terror
Sanctuary cities	Extreme vetting
Black Lives Matter	Blue Lives Matter
Rachel Maddow	Megyn Kelly
Feel the Bern	"Feel the Donald"
"What difference, at this point, does it make?"	Pat Smith, Gold Star Mom
"You didn't build that"	"You built that"
Dixie Chicks	Zac Brown Band
President Mahmoud Abbas	Justice Clarence Thomas
Participation trophies	Scoreboards
Greek exceptionalism	American exceptionalism
Multiculturalism	Assimulation
Chris Matthews	Sean Hannity
Rev. Jeremiah Wright	Rev. Billy Graham
Speaker Nancy Pelosi	Speaker Paul Ryan
Coach Phil Jackson	Coach Bobby Knight
Coastal America	Flyover America

"I'm with her"   "Make America Great Again"
Fahrenheit 9/11   *American Sniper*
Clinton State Department   Tony Soprano
Overseas contingency operation   War

The New York Times   *The Wall Street Journal*
Mayor Bill de Blasio   Mayor Rudy Guiliani
Solyndra   Keystone
Sean Penn   Clint Eastwood
"Happy Holidays"   "Merry Christmas"

I ended one of my 2013 columns with the following observations:

For those who chose the left column more than half the time, you may safely identify as a Democrat. Those of you who leaned right more times than not will most likely feel at home with the GOP.

For the few of you who ended up exactly half and half, you are that rare breed known as the true moderate. Without doubt, the pollsters will flock to your door every election cycle; you are the holy grail of "swing voters" ripe for participation in an endless stream of cable television focus groups.

But buyer beware: "They" say the only things found in the middle of the road are straight white lines and dead animals. In today's hyper-partisan Washington, you might add a smattering of dead politicians of a certain moderate bent.

Seems some things don't change much.

News from the Future

October 27, 2016, *Washington Examiner*

Just imagine if all your wishes came true.

In a surprise announcement, the House Democratic leadership (present and former) took full responsibility for the historic housing bubble and recession of 2008–10. "Our bad," asserted former Congressman Barney Frank.

"We just forgot that threatening the banks into underwriting mortgages for those with no income and bad credit scores could backfire...and how were we supposed to know the Clinton administration would get Fannie and Freddie to lower their underwriting standards at the same time?"

Attorney General Maxine Waters joined in the apology, while delivering personal "thank you" notes to the same banks that President Obama himself had asked for help from during the crisis. "It was just a simple case of seeing all that green," explained the AG. "It was so easy to demonize those greedy Republican bankers that we overlooked the fact we helped cause this mess in the first place."

The San Francisco City Council today repudiated its "sanctuary city" status and issued a "heartfelt apology" for its "unfortunate actions" in support of "illegal behavior."

"We plead 'temporary insanity,'" commented Mayor Rev. Jesse Jackson, citing the city's proximity to Berkeley as the likely cause of its progressive infatuation.

"In retrospect, the chutzpah it took to think we could unilaterally thumb our noses at federal law leaves me speechless," added the second-term mayor. Jackson went on to bemoan how illegal immigration disproportionately hurts African American laborers—especially those at the bottom of the economic ladder. Mayor Jackson was later seen at a "Make San Francisco Great Again" rally attended by President Trump.

Also of note, the San Francisco school system voted to reinstate a mandatory "Pledge of Allegiance" and "morning prayer" in its school-day curriculum. "We decided a bit of patriotism and values education might not be so bad," commented School Board President Saul Alinsky. "Things haven't exactly improved since we removed God from our classrooms."

Third-term President Hillary Clinton today produced the final batch of mistakenly "deleted," "lost," "didn't remember," or "somehow survived a sledgehammer" emails from her tenure at the State Department. The president also issued an apology for the appearance of "pay-for-play" favors that benefited certain Clinton Foundation contributors.

In explaining her "mea culpa," the president pointed out that she and her husband had "run Arkansas the same way—if you know what I mean...so we thought to do the same thing at Foggy Bottom. Who knew we were supposed to follow the rules?"

An angry Minority Leader Stephanie McMahon, R-Conn., dismissed the long-sought apology as "phonier than a 'Monday Night Raw' championship bout." A nonplussed Clinton responded, "What difference, at this point, does it make?"

The Clinton administration today sent two Navy cruisers full of cash to Iran in what was called the final payment due and owing for America's "blatant imperialism" and "wrongful actions against revolutionary Islamic governments...since the beginning of time."

The money was accompanied by a "letter of apology" from the American people and included a promise to eliminate all aid directed to the "warmongering" state of Israel, America's former ally in the Middle East.

President Hillary Clinton signed a number of new bills into law today, including a new criminal statute directed to those who insist on using "Merry Christmas" during the winter solstice.

"Such incendiary language has no place in this multicultural land," opined the president. The newly redesignated "Department of Fairness, Sensitivity, Egalitarianism, Tolerance, Acceptance, and No Privilege Whatsoever" promised to "prosecute any remaining remnants of the prohibited holiday...jolly fat guys with beards notwithstanding..."

A coalition of civil rights groups has filed suit against the United States government, claiming the proliferation of photo identification requirements violates the constitutional rights of 12 million illegal aliens.

The American Civil Liberties Union (lead plaintiff) issued the following statement: "Photo identification requirements are always discriminatory—whether one is entering a public building, purchasing allergy medicine, or visiting the attorney general herself....How else are our uninvited, illegal friends supposed to live here if our racist society requires them to identify themselves?"

Attorney General Debbie Wasserman Schultz praised the lawsuit, promising to eliminate all required forms of personal identification—with the exception of those seeking to enter the Department of Justice.

Approximately one hundred Young Republicans stormed the office of Dartmouth University president Elizabeth Warren today. No damage was reported. The intruders appeared to be from a coalition of groups, including "The College Republicans," "Junior Achievement," and "The Junior League."

A list of demands was soon issued, including an end to "free" tuition and grade inflation, a return to the school's original nickname—"Indians"—and restoration of "God" as an acceptable noun in the school's speech code-approved "Hymns in Chapel Services."

Dartmouth provost and former U.S. Senator Bernie Sanders decried the invasion, calling the protesters' demands for free speech and respectful discussion "dangerous—really a hate crime, especially at an academic institution."

NFL Commissioner Gloria Steinem today outlawed the "shotgun and pistol" formations.

"Henceforth, these formations will be known as, 'we're probably gonna pass,' " stated the new commish. She also promised to eliminate "other masculine, gratuitously violent" terminology from the game. Assistant Commissioner Cher confirmed a number of recently opened investigations, and openly questioned the concept of a "man-to-man" defense, "for obvious reasons."

Mission Accomplished, Comrade

May 18, 2017, *Washington Examiner*

Big news! Look what I found in a plain manila envelope buried in a pumpkin patch in Carroll County, Maryland, last week:

MEMO
To: V. Putin
From: "Special Team USA"
Date: November 9, 2016

Mr. President—

Well, we did it. Against all odds, we pulled out all the stops and ended the Clinton dynasty.

Your plan worked to perfection—so well in fact that we believe at some point in the next year, the Democrats will blame the Republicans for being in cahoots with us. I'm not kidding. Our agents report that the Democrats are in such a state of denial that they have no idea about our deep infiltration into the Democratic National Committee and Clinton Campaign.

Please allow us to brag a bit about our successful operation.

First, we could not have pulled this off without our agents convincing the Secretary of State that she needed to set up an offline email operation—complete with an independent server. We at first thought it to be too outlandish an idea, but she bought it hook, line, and sinker. Talk about buying in; she had thought of it before we even brought it up. She even came up with the idea to hide the server at her Chappaqua, NY, home.

It was all downhill from there. Our agents then leaked the arrangement to the media—and just sat back and watched her offer up one phony explanation after another until even *she* got confused from telling so many versions. After a while, even CNN stopped believing her!

Special commendation to our WikiLeaks Liaison Section, who found and leaked John Podesta's emails showing his frustration with Hillary's email shenanigans. By the way, this group also spilled the beans on how Clinton's iPhone was sledgehammered into a million pieces—a stunt right out of the KGB playbook!

Truth be told, even our WikiLeaks operatives' efforts paled in comparison to the excellence of our new "Millennial Group." Recall they are the twentysomethings who got themselves hired in the campaign's analytics department. Then they convinced the Clinton campaign that it need not campaign in the upper Midwest, i.e., the so-called impregnable "Blue Wall."

Note that these college kids pressed the case against the strong opposition of former President Clinton (who proved to be a constant thorn in their side). He knew the economic angst in the heartland and never missed an opportunity to alert his wife's campaign to the facts. Alas, our fake models of a huge millennial/minority turnout played precisely into the mind-set of the Democratic establishment. Our agents even had them "expanding the map" just a week out from election day.

Special kudos to our network of campus agents. These young comrades have worked tirelessly to turn American colleges and universities into little laboratories of progressive thought—so far left that even Bernie Sanders and Elizabeth Warren were seen as serious alternatives to Mrs. Clinton. Fortunately, the Sanders and Warren threat turned Clinton *further* left. Long gone was the moderate of 2008. Happily, her new strategy adopted every plank in the progressive playbook—so far outside the mainstream that we could predict with certainty that places like Pittsburgh and western Pennsylvania would move deep red—and boy, did they! Clinton was crushed in white working-class neighborhoods all across the Rust Belt.

Parenthetically, our campaign to turn college millennials against capitalism, free speech, Fox News, and their parents' values is meeting with spectacular success—although I must admit it is a bit like taking candy from a baby, so to speak. Progressive wing nut college administrators are always the first to jump on any anti-American (or -Israeli) bandwagon we start. Their brethren in the faculty gleefully pile on. Incredibly, some universities are hiring "sensitivity police" to monitor "micro-aggressions" committed by bourgeois Republicans against our uber-sensitive young snowflakes. Who said "participation trophies" don't work?! And more good news: Our field agents report that soon we will (finally) reach our goal of eliminating American history and basic economics from core requirements at America's colleges and universities.

Finally, a huge shout-out to our "Identity Politics" group. As you know, these agents have so infiltrated the Democratic Party's grassroots that periodic calls for moderation from the party's few moderates are like trees falling in the forest—nobody hears them. We can only marvel at their success. They have taken a party once identified with America's melting pot–believing working class and turned it into a loose confederation of self-styled victims and culture warriors. Just think—this group was able to get a United States Senator and presidential candidate who once opposed special driver's licenses for illegal aliens to openly support sanctuary cities—you know, those cities and towns that proudly oppose federal law enforcement—even when dangerous felons are on the loose. That, my dear president, is what we call serious growth!

Hopefully, all of our Washington, DC, agents will be able to keep a straight face as the "investigation" into the Trump-Russia connection continues. Ha! If they only knew.

Thinking About What Might Have Been

April 7, 2017, *Washington Examiner*

That Barack Obama transformed America is without doubt; by just about any measure the country moved left during his tenure. Social permissiveness and political correctness ruled the day. But such heady progress is now in the distant past—thanks to one Donald J. Trump. How far down the progressive highway could it have gone? How close to the edge did we get? The answer: real far and real close. Just take a glance at these news reports from what could have been your future:

- Former Vice President Al Gore introduced the latest sequel to *An Inconvenient Truth* at the 2035 Sundance Film Festival. The new movie follows previous releases *An Inconvenient Sequel* (2017), *Inconvenient Blizzards Mean We're in Real Trouble* (2022), *Sometimes Computer Models Can Be Inconvenient* (2028), *I Think I Got It Right This Time* (2031), and his new release, *I Should Have Stuck with Tipper on That Record Label Warning Gig*. On a somber note, Mr. Gore's scheduled press conference was postponed when a spring snowstorm grounded his private jet in Cancún, Mexico.

- The University of California at Berkeley officially changed its name to "Che Guevara University" in honor of the slain Cuban revolutionary. School historian Abbie Hoffman noted that Guevara's continuing popularity is reflected in a clothing line that has led the university's retail sales for the past fifty-three years. Hoffman added, "This honor is long overdue. Although Colin Kaepernick's 'Oops, I fumbled the snap' hoodies are hot right now, Che remains 'the man' on this campus. You could see the momentum building—first the football stadium was renamed 'Nike / Ho Chi Minh Field,' then the basketball arena 'Reebok/Angela Davis Fieldhouse,' next, the baseball complex became 'Fidel's Field,' and who can forget our new undergraduate housing complex—'HUD/Sanctuary City.'" Newly elected university president Lois Lerner (recently released from the witness protection program) assured concerned alumni that the name change would not impact the school's nonprofit status. "I know my way around the nonprofit world—if you know what I mean," noted Ms. Lerner.

- A disconsolate Lena Dunham returned to America today after an aborted stay in the workers' paradise of Venezuela. The actress had been the lone Hollywood star to follow through on a promise to leave the country after President-for-Life Trump unilaterally suspended the 12th Amendment in 2023. "I know it's supposed to be a socialist utopia, but that place is miserable. Limo service is choppy, the spas are nasty, and my local Starbucks ran out of gingerbread lattes at Christmas," added Dunham. The progressive star will next look to make a new home in another workers' paradise—North Korea. Miss Dunham expressed excitement at the prospect, but wondered if Kim Jong-un had included *Girls* on Pyongyang's basic cable package.

- California Governor Jerry Brown announced that his state's marginal tax rate has now reached 100 percent. "Thank God we finally eclipsed Venezuela. It's been quite a journey," noted the eight-term executive. Shortly thereafter, the California Chamber of Commerce confirmed it had lost its last member, a fully automated Wendy's located on the outskirts of San Jose—to Las Vegas, Nevada. Brown was nonplussed by the chamber's news, noting that the California legislature had previously outlawed "immoral corporate profits" by raising the state minimum wage to $49 per hour.

- A beaming Eric Holder today formally assumed the presidency of a new Chicago-based community college dedicated to the art of "community organizing." "ACORN College" will be dedicated as a nuclear-free zone and conveniently located next to several large multinational banks—"the better to practice demonstration techniques against profiteering money changers," according to the school's mission statement.

  Course offerings to be taught by a variety of big-name lecturers were also announced. Among the most popular: "Credit Rating; What Credit Rating?" (Professors C. Dodd and B. Frank); "How to Shake Down a Small Business in 12 Easy Steps" (ACORN faculty); "Misunderstood: From Uncle Joe to Mao to Raúl" (Professor E. Warren); "The Private Sector Is WAY Overrated" (Professor B. Sanders); and "Who Needs Congress Anyway?" (guest lecturer, B. Obama).

  But all was not peaceful on the ACORN campus after university provost Madonna decided that photo IDs would henceforth be required of all students. In response, groups of protesters broke into Mr. Holder's office chanting, "Not my president" and "You can't make me, I'm illegal" until a "sensitivity ombudsman" from the campus "Trigger Warnings and Microaggressions Enforcement Bureau" showed up to detain Ms. Madonna on charges of "insufficient empathy in a safe zone." Fortunately, president Holder was able to negotiate the provost's freedom after agreeing to a series of student demands, including the imposition of an "unfair American privilege fee" on natural-born students and designation of the school as a First Amendment-Free Zone.

- The semi-autonomous territories of California and New York today announced their new constitutions to online customers at the 238,000 Starbucks locations in the twin venues. A new "à la carte" legal framework will allow each legislature to "pick

219

and choose" the constitutional amendments they will recognize. 2046's election results showed voters in the respective states accepting the 3rd through 8th, 11th, 13th, 16th, 19th, and 24th Amendments. As expected, the law formerly known as "the 2nd Amendment" failed to garner even a single vote. In a mild surprise, the former "1st Amendment" was voted down 59–41 percent, with entire college towns rejecting the concept of free speech as a violation of local speech codes. The "à la carte" process is said to date back thirty years, to a time when cities and states began to reject the concept of what was then known as "citizenship" through the adoption of so-called "sanctuary cities"—a now illegal "hate phrase" per President Warren's newly issued "Forbidden Word" list.

Conclusion

The Trump administration was only five weeks old when initial public opinion polls reflected a historic low of 44 percent approval. The mainstream media reported the bad news with banner headlines. There had, in fact, been no honeymoon for the "disrupter-in-chief." Then Mr. Trump gave an extraordinarily strong performance at his first appearance before a joint session of Congress. The speech was a hit; overnight polling showed strong support for the new president's no-holds-barred pitch on behalf of his "America First" agenda. Just like that, Republicans were (again) jubilant, and Democrats upset, at this jolting reminder of their new reality.

The best way to describe a Trump-era status quo is to understand there is no such thing. The non-politician president continues to rewrite the manual—indeed, tear it up on occasion. He and his *Breitbart* buddy (and former staffer), Steve Bannon, willingly and happily claim the disrupter mantle. They believe disrespect for political convention gave Mr. Trump the presidency. Neither seems able (or willing) to change course. It is a trait that likely caused Mr. Bannon's dismissal after nearly eight months on the job.

On the ground this means daily (or more) White House tweets will continue; that regular fistfights with left-leaning news outlets will also continue; that internecine grievances large and petty will regularly occupy the president's time and energy; and that the same sometimes unfocused man is fully capable of leading a mass movement of people intent on bringing fundamental change to our politics.

Meanwhile, the other side of the aisle appears intent on slogging down the hard left highway—what is now a one-lane progressive road. Its once powerful "Blue Dogs" are an endangered species as moderation has been sentenced to the dustbin of history. Accordingly, there is *no way* progressives could accept the notion that 2016 was a rejection of Obama-style progressivism. Rather, they cling to the belief that Hillary Clinton was a flawed candidate, victimized by Vladimir Putin, James Comey (when he was the bad guy), and millions of secret misogynists who would not indulge the notion of a female president. The election of the hard-left Tom Perez to the chairmanship of the Democratic National Committee (and his appointment of the equally far-left Keith Ellison as his deputy) reflect this path. Both men are "all in" for the American version of a shadow government in waiting, led by the former two-term president of the United States. For the left, this means a return to grassroots organizing and agitating—activities perfected by Mr. Obama and his acolytes.

For the professional grievance industry, these are the best and worst of times. On the upside, they could not have a more convenient boogeyman to attack. For them, Donald Trump is the archetypical arrogant capitalist ready and willing to serve the interests of all those greedy Wall Street bankers. Adding to the vitriol is a never-ending list of missteps, faux pas, scandals, and misstatements that are invariably seen as Trump's "end of days." Just think about the breathless anticipation that followed media bombshells of serial womanizing, sexual harassment, unpaid Atlantic City vendors, Billy Bush, poor debate performances, the belittling of fellow Republican political contenders, and Twitter wars with everyone from Rosie O'Donnell to Joe Scarborough to the Pope. For the left, this is the stuff of strong fundraising and glorious protests. And this crowd really knows how to protest!.

But the day-to-day downside is equally dramatic. The nightmare of Republican-dominated government is always front and center— and precious little is to their liking. Now these Obama-ites must live with Justice Neil Gorsuch and the return of a 5–4 conservative majority. Also on a disquieting agenda: border security, tax cuts, regulatory downsizing, a replaced (or at least tweaked) Obamacare, increased military spending, domestic spending cuts, rapprochement with Israel's right-wing government, a reborn American nationalism, and a fossil fuel rebirth. All are facts of their new reality. Is it any wonder why so many have taken to the streets or reached new lows of illiberal protest on our college campuses?

Truth be told, ugly does not begin to describe Washington's (or the country's) political divide. Partisanship of the worst kind has disabled "regular order" in Congress. Too many "safe seats" make negotiation or compromise impossible. Moderates of both parties were last seen on the back of milk cartons. Social media feeds the vitriol by the minute. The public cringes, but watches....

The first year of the Trump administration accurately reflected the upheaval. The brutal campaign of 2016 seemingly never stopped. The president continued to schedule campaign-style rallies while the Democrats jumped on every real or falsely reported Trump misstep to further degrade the man and his administration. Some allege Trump himself is the primary instigator of the unpleasantness. Indeed, candidate Trump's practice of belittling his GOP competitors (e.g., "Little Marco," "Low-Energy Jeb," and "Lying Ted") did not exactly convey a sense of collegiality among his peers. Colorful and often personal tweets targeted at political antagonists only add to the indictment. That others have adopted this hostile style should come as no surprise.

These pundits raise a valid point: Candidate Trump brought a brash, dismissive style that violated traditional norms of political discourse. But it is far too easy to attribute today's poisoned environment to simply a byproduct of one businessman president's fondness for Twitter blasts and personal attacks. The coarsening of our politics (and culture) has been ongoing for decades. Recall the vitriol of the Clarence Thomas hearings, or Robert Bork's transformation into a verb. Indeed, the same hand grenades and kitchen sinks utilized by today's angry progressives were also thrown at Ronald Reagan and George W. Bush. The explanation for such emotionalism never changes: Anyone carrying the moniker of conservative and occupying a leadership position will be viewed by the media intelligentsia as a threat—and accordingly demonized.

Herein, then, is the genesis of the chants, parades, campus riots, intelligence agency leaks, Broadway insults, and endless Russian hacking narratives. You see, this generation of progressives got a taste—eight sweet years of Obama-inspired cultural and economic transformation—and they liked it. They simply do not want it to end. How ironic then that such a vision could lead to Donald Trump.

I often conclude my public lectures by pointing out the "unmet needs" paradox of modern progressive thought. I remind audiences how Vice President Biden had excused the failure of his administration's $1.2 trillion stimulus package by claiming that it just wasn't big enough, and that President Obama wistfully observed that Baltimore burned in the spring of 2015 because the government had not spent enough on America's inner cities. These are only two examples (among many) reflecting the popular progressive view that just a few more dollars will fix our unmet needs. Of course, the list of such needs is endless—hence socialism's circular logic. How useful—a paradigm that can *never* be disproved and always sounds so good when you say it really fast. No wonder socialism appeals to young people who have never experienced it.

On the other side are the "Never Trumpers" and other disillusioned conservatives ready, willing, and able to continue their opposition to the new administration. They see the president as too abrasive, too flawed, too self-absorbed to be another Reagan. For this crowd, the differences are stark: Where Reagan used personal warmth, humor, and empathy to compete, the one-trick pony Trump brings only a sledgehammer. They also see Trump's daily, sometimes gratuitous, war of words as counterproductive—as evidence of an unfocused executive too preoccupied with petty fights and personal slights to get things done. In a word, they view Trump as too *exhausting*, sure to burn up so much goodwill that little will remain after four long years.

* * *

Six months into the Trump presidency I was asked to appear at a Perryville, Maryland, bridge dedication in honor of a fallen Marine who had lost his life in Iraq. I humbly accepted, as the mother of the Marine (Mrs. Martina Burger) had been a guest at one of the private ceremonies I had hosted for families of killed and wounded Maryland soldiers during my tenure as governor of Maryland.

I arrived late but was able to talk with Mrs. Burger and many of the assembled guests for the better part of an hour. The audience was largely made up of former Marines, Maryland state troopers, local police, members of the American Legion, and local business leaders. All were present to celebrate the life of a fallen American hero—which was accomplished in grand style. This is what small communities do to acknowledge local heroes.

But it was the political talk that made such a strong impression on me, primarily the emotional statements of support for one Donald J. Trump. Interestingly, this was during a time the president's approval ratings had plummeted to the mid-30s, Obamacare "repeal and replace" was stuck in the Senate, and he had just been blistered by the media for an insulting tweet directed at MSNBC *Morning Joe* co-anchor Mika Brzezinski.

You would not have known that Mr. Trump's poll numbers were depressed by the comments of those assembled, however. Quite the

contrary—*this group was fired up*. They finally had a president willing
to say all the things they could only think. It struck me that this was
the Trump base in all its glory—and anger—still fully energized seven
choppy months after a historic election upset. The widely analyzed
demographics of the Trump coalition were accurately reflected here:
a mix of white working- and middle-class Republicans and Democrats
fearful of losing their culture and their (American) dream. This group
did not particularly care that incessant tweeting kept throwing the
president off message. They just loved the happy-warrior way he con-
tinually threw bricks at the Washington elites.

* * *

For Republicans, like it or not, Mr. Trump is the only game in town.
Flaws or not, he is the lead dog. He sets the agenda. He decides which
battles to fight. He is best positioned to expose the false promises of
progressives. (After all, their overreaching gave the GOP the presidency in the first place.) And those who deem this a vital mission must
do their part to help.

Whether this unorthodox style will result in a successful presidency (and/or a permanent working-class realignment) will play out
over the remainder of DJT's term. Conventional wisdom says no—
steep institutional opposition and needless drama will in the end prove
too much for even Donald Trump to sustain. The "Donald Express" will
ultimately run out of fuel. The establishment's old rule book will suddenly revert to form.

Yet my eyes and ears tell me something far different. *Obama II* and
Trump I have provided me a front-row seat to the once inconceivable
welcome wagon Middle America has set out for its imperfect mes-
senger. These good folks are enjoying the unexpected ride—as is their
leader.

Words still count. Ideas still matter. Freedom of thought, word,
and deed still define us. These freedoms help expose the shallowness

Conclusion

of progressive thought, and daily engagement is required for such a worthy endeavor.

And no, the vast majority of us did *not* see this one coming, but welcome to history. And thanks for taking the time to read my take on the life and times of the good ole U.S. of A. during the always exciting reign of Donald J. Trump.

Epilogue

The most difficult aspect of any book starring Donald Trump is figuring out where, when, and how to stop. The man is a nonstop news machine. He dominates every media cycle by design, or otherwise. He lives the old cliché, "There is no such thing as bad press." His political base cannot get enough of it. His opponents have yet to understand how he could get elected in the first place.

Indeed, the first year of the Trump era saw the American left descend ever deeper into resistance mode. Progressive social media ran stories of the president's alleged mental illnesses. A few Congressional Democrats talked openly of impeachment. Articles were indeed filed in November, presumably to commemorate the one-year anniversary of Trump's victory. Their like-minded brethren in the media assumed a relentlessly anti-Trump messaging strategy, all the while proving themselves quite flexible in going about their business. To wit, what was once an all-encompassing Russian collusion narrative seemingly overnight gave way to an "alt-right" racist narrative without skipping a beat. Alas, few seemed to notice as the bottom line never changed: Trump must go.

For his part, the president proved predictably unpredictable. Strong performances were frequently overtaken by stream-of-consciousness Twitter blasts. Senior advisers—including a chief of staff—came and went from a West Wing revolving door. Attorney

Epilogue

General Jeff Sessions, a loyal ally, was castigated for recusing himself from the Russia investigation. Majority Leader Mitch McConnell suffered a similar fate for failing to pass an Obamacare replacement (but accomplished a quick comeback when substantial progress was made on Mr. Trump's signature tax reform proposal). Senior staff and cabinet secretaries were openly critical of a too tepid response to Charlottesville race agitators. But sabre rattling threats from Kim Jong-un were met with equally aggressive responses from a president unaccustomed to being threatened—or backing down.

It was all so...different. Herein was a free agent leader. Strategy sessions with the GOP leadership were few and far between, especially after the Senate's disappointing performance on "repeal and replace." Then, a debt ceiling/temporary spending deal was struck with the Democrats alone. Alas, Republican hurt feelings were of no consequence. Primetime bully pulpit addresses were rare, but he would give daily light (and tweet) to whatever thoughts were running through his head at the time. Was it salesmanship? Yep. The art of the deal? Sometimes. A grand design? On major issues, yes. Did it set lefty Trump haters and Republican establishment types off their rockers? You betcha.

As you attempt to digest the daily fire hose of events that defines the Trump era, one piece of advice: *Focus on the big stuff*—the 180-degree end of Obama-era stuff—and try mightily not to sweat the small stuff. Bet you couldn't see the small stuff coming anyway....

Acknowledgments

The list of essential people required to get my books completed in an orderly and timely manner has not changed very much over time. This is indeed a blessing I do not take for granted. And so a fourth round of kudos is due to the following individuals who make it all happen:

Kendel Ehrlich Wife, best friend, unyielding defender of her husband, and protector of all things Ehrlich. She runs the family—and thereby allows me to engage my writing with the necessary peace of mind.

Chris Massoni Administrative assistant and friend for the past twenty-three years. She is one of the very few individuals on earth able to offer edits to my drafts—most of which are incorporated into the final product.

Greg Massoni Former press secretary, loyal friend, and publicist emeritus of all things Ehrlich over the past fifteen years. The definition of unconditional friendship.

Professor Richard Vatz Good friend and the other professional with the credibility to offer ideas and propose edits. A master of political rhetoric and beloved professor at Towson University.

Denny Mather Close friend and respected thinker regarding the state of American health care. He is one of the few Americans to have actually read "The Affordable Care Act."

Jim Pettit Former staffer, friend, and deep thinker on the causes and solutions associated with homelessness and poverty.

Stephanie Krikorian Excellent editor and sometimes agent. Always willing to step up for the team.

Elaine Pevenstein Godmother of all things "Ehrlich Inc."